Comparative Law of Contracts

Carolina Academic Press
Comparative Law Series

Michael Louis Corrado
Series Editor

Comparative Constitutional Review
Cases and Materials
Michael Louis Corrado

Comparative Law: An Introduction
Vivian Grosswald Curran

Comparative Consumer Bankruptcy
Jason Kilborn

Comparative Law of Contracts
Alain Levasseur

Comparative Criminal Procedure, Second Edition
Stephen C. Thaman

Comparative Human Rights Law, Vol. 1:
Expression, Association, Religion
A. Mark Weisburd

Comparative Human Rights Law, Vol. 2:
Detention, Prosecution, Capital Punishment
A. Mark Weisburd

Comparative Law of Contracts

Cases and Materials

Alain A. Levasseur
Hermann Moyse, Sr. Professor of Law
Director, European Studies
LSU Law Center

CAROLINA ACADEMIC PRESS
Durham, North Carolina

Library of Congress Cataloging-in-Publication Data

Levasseur, Alain A.
  Comparative law of contracts : cases and materials / by Alain A.
Levasseur.
      p. cm.
  Includes bibliographical references and index.
  ISBN 13: 978-1-59460-198-9 / ISBN 10: 1-59460-198-4 (alk. paper)
  1. Contracts. 2. Comparative law. 3. Contracts--Cases. I. Title.

  K840.L48 2008
  346.02--dc22

2008001759

Carolina Academic Press
700 Kent Street
Durham, North Carolina 27701
Telephone (919) 489-7486
Fax (919) 493-5668
www.cap-press.com
Printed in the United States of America

for
Francis, Gabriel, John Paul, Libby Kate

Contents

Part I
Formation of Contracts

Acknowledgments and Permissions

We are grateful to the following publishers for their permission to reprint excerpts from the following:

Oxford University Press for "An Introduction to the Law of Contract" (1995) by P.S. Atiyah, 4th edition, pages 124, 157–160, 167–169. Permission granted: October 14, 2007.

LexisNexis Butterworths for "The Law of Contract" 3rd edition (2007). Permission granted: August 24, 2007.

Adapted with the permission of Aspen Publishers from Allan Farnsworth, "Contracts," 4th edition, pages p. 3–4, 14, 47–48, 53, 57, 70, 108, 110–112, 114–115,145, 170, 189, 501, 535–540, 547–553, 599, 601, 619, 625, 634, 642, 729, 739, 757. 2004. Permission granted: August 29, 2007.

Reprinted from "The Law of Contracts," Calamari and Perillo, 4th edition, 1998 with permission of Thompson West. Permission granted: August 24, 2007.

"Contracts," G.H. Trietel, 1987, Sweet & Maxwell. Permission granted: October 10, 2007.

Introduction

Comparative law of contract or Comparative law of contracts? What difference does the letter "s" bring to the alternative? Actually, this single letter "s" is, to a large extent, illustrative of the different approaches of the common law system and of the civil law system to one and the same legal concept of "obligation," or bond of law, created by human will. Whereas, on the one hand, the civil law system has developed or built a "theory of contract" and, thus, a "law of contract" in the singular, as an all encompassing legal framework elaborated on the logic of an inductive reasoning process based on a variety of existing contracts, be they to give, to do or not to do something..., on the other hand the common law system still refers to "contracts," hence the "law of contracts." In a way, therefore, the common law is not concerned with the possible existence of a single or universal legal concept of "contract," as an abstract entity, responding to its own legal features which would then be common to all "contracts."

Yet both the common law of <u>contracts</u> and the civil law of <u>contract</u> can trace their "roots" to the law of contracts in Roman law. In the course of history the two systems will part ways and adopt, here and there, different legal approaches to solving, however, the same practical issues created by the same need to regulate all sorts of transactions arising from the interactions of men whether they operate in a common law system or in a civil law system. If the civil law has taken more a legislative and regulatory approach, under the form of codification, harmonization and legislation, the common law has taken a more praetorian approach as reflected in the jurisprudence of the courts of common law. Still, there is no harmonized or uniform contract law gathering together the civil law jurisdictions, even within the European Union, under one single civil law of contract. As we shall see in the following chapters there exist differences between civil law jurisdictions and between the latter and the common law jurisdictions. Reconciliations between all these jurisdictions is still a long way in the distant future! Yet many of the solutions to the legal problems are the same.

We will attempt, first, to illustrate these two fundamentally different approaches of the civil law and the common law by comparing some identical elements required for the formation of a binding contract in both legal systems. (Part I). In a second Part, we will focus on some effects of contracts and some remedies available in the event of a breach of a contract. (Part II). However, a brief historical survey of the law of contract or contracts in Roman law, in the civil law and in the common law and a survey of the concepts of "juridical acts" and "contracts" are a necessary preliminary step in this comparative analysis.

Abbreviations

Louisiana Civil Code: La. Civ. C. [West Publishing Company]

Louisiana Revised Statutes: La. R. S. [West Publishing Company]

Louisiana Law Review: La. L. Rev.

French Civil Code: Fr. Civ. C. [Code Dalloz]

Civil Code of Québec: C.C.Q. [Wilson & Lafleur Ltée]

German Civil Code: BGB [juris GmbH, Saarbrücken]

Restatement of the Law Second Contracts 2d: Restatement, 2d [The American Law Institute]

Uniform Commercial Code: UCC [Foundation Press]

The Unidroit Principles in Practice: UNIDROIT Principles [Transnational Publishers]

United Nations Convention on Contracts for the International Sale of Goods: CISG [Center for International Legal Education, University of Pittsburgh School of Law]

Swiss Federal Code of Obligations: Sw. Fed. C.O. [Wettstein]

Swiss Civil Code: Sw. Civ. C. [ReMaK Verlag Zürich]

Italian Civil Code: It. Civ. C. [Oceana Publications, Inc.]

Materials Cited

E. Allan Farnsworth, Contracts, Fourth Edition, Aspen 2004

G.H. Treitel, Q.C., The Law of Contract, Seventh Edition, Stevens and Sons, 1987

LexisNexis Butterworths, The Law of Contract, Third Edition, 2007

P.S. Atiyah, An Introduction to The Law of Contract, Fourth Edition, Clarendon Press, 1989

Principles of European Contract Law, Kluwer Law International, 2000.

Comparative Law of Contracts

Chapter One

Historical Survey

A. Roman Law Origins

The Latin verb "*obligare*" has a meaning equivalent to the English verb "to bind." One can read this Latin word in the modern English word "ligament" which has for its function to bind two or more bones in our body. The Latin word "*obligatio*" meant to refer both to the right that existed on one side of a legal relationship and the duty that existed on the other side of it; it was intended to be a bond of law or "*vinculum juris.*"[1]

Justinian:
Obligatio est juris vinculum, ...

Let us now pass to obligations. An obligation is the chain of the law, ...

Gaius:
88. Let us now proceed to obligations. These are divided into two main species: for every obligation arises either from contract or from delict.

Under the *jus civile*[2] this bond of law could arise from two main sources: either *ex contractu* (out of a contract) or *ex delicto* (out of a delict). Such was

---

1. The Institutes of Justinian with notes by Thomas Cooper, Esq., Philadelphia, 1812. Lib. III.Tit.XIV. De Obligationibus: " ... An obligation is the chain of the law, by which we are necessarily bound to make some payment, according to the laws of our country.

2. The Institutes of Justinian, (supra note 1): Lib. Tit.II. " Jus autem civile ..." "Civil law is distinguished from the law of nations, because every community governed by laws, uses partly its own and partly the laws which are common to all mankind. That law, which a people enacts for its own government, is called the civil law of that people ...".

the basic classical Roman law concept of obligation. Where there was a gap in the *jus civile*, the Roman praetor would provide for those situations not covered specifically by the *jus civile*. The praetor created remedies or actions in those situations where an obligation could be said to arise *quasi ex contractu* (out of a relationship that looked almost like a contract) or *quasi ex delicto* (almost like a delict). Such was the status of Roman law in the VIth century as it was incorporated in Justinian's Institutes.[3]

1. Obligations are primarily divided into two kinds, civil and praetorian.

2. The second or subsequent division of obligations is four fold: by contract (*ex contractu*), by quasi-contract (*quasi ex contractu*), by malefeasance (*ex maleficio*) and by quasi-malefeasance (*quasi ex maleficio).*

In the legal systems of several jurisdictions (France, Germany, Italy, Québec, ...) which belong to the civil law tradition, we find the same basic division of the sources of obligations: the French civil Code (Book III contracts, *quasi contracts, delicts, quasi delicts*); the Louisiana Civil Code (Book III, Tit.III, Art. 1757); the Bürgerliches Gesetzbuch, (BGB), (Book II 2nd Sect, 7th Sect. Titles 24, 25). At common law we have, basically, two elements of the same general division of obligations between "Contracts" and "Torts." With respect to obligations arising *quasi ex contractu*, the common law would placed them, in general, under "Restitution."

This formal identity of the sources of obligations, in contracts in particular, is very limited in its scope. It actually hides very different historical developments as regards the very concept of "contract."

In Roman law, the verb "*contrahere*" (the etymological root of contract) meant to "effect, to perpetrate, to bring oneself." For example, one could '*contrahere nuptias*' (enter into a marriage) or '*contrahere amicitium*' (enter into a bond of friendship).

Contrahere, as such, did not mean to make a contract. The word "contractus" appeared later, when it was devised by lawyers during the late Republic. It was then used in connection with another word, as illustrated above with respect to *contrahere*. For example: *contractus emptionis* was the making of a contract of purchase and sale.

As the word "*contractus*" was used repeatedly in conjunction with other words describing different actions, it ended up taking an identity of its own so as to mean a "contract" or an agreement entered into by the parties to it so

---

3. Id. Lib. III. Tit. XIV.

as to create an obligation. That obligation itself would find its identity in specific words such as "to buy," as in "*emptio*," or to enter into a "buy" by one party and a "sell," or "*venditio*," by another party so as to create a contract of sale: "*emptio-venditio.*"[4] But Roman law did not know, as the common law does not know either, a general theory of contract. Rather, there existed a variety of 'contracts.'

In this respect, we find in Gaius' Institutes an illustration of a specific feature of the civil law which is the formulation and the articulation of "classifications" or "categorizations" of legal institutions. There is, in the civil law tradition, a Cartesian or systematic method of thinking and analyzing legal relationships which is foreign to the common law.[5] The Roman jurists already displayed this ability at organizing and structuring practical economic, commercial, financial relationships into contractual 'concepts' which became somewhat abstract in their legal scheme. For example, in Gaius Institutes and Justinian's Institutes, we find a reference to four general kinds of contractual obligations into which all contracts which meet certain identified requirements will fall. These four general kinds of contracts are: real contractual obligations (*re contrahitur obligatio*)[6]; verbal or oral contractual obligations (*verbis obligatio*)[7]; literal contractual obligations (*De Literarum Obligationibus*): the existence of a form of writing and a document of acknowledgment were required); consensual contractual obligations (*De Obligationibus ex consensu*).[8]

Parties to a contract could have intended to enter into a contract somewhat different from the existing kinds of contracts. They could do so provided they worked out the special arrangements they wanted to include in a particular type of contract in such a manner that they would not change the legal nature of that contract. Otherwise the parties could lose the benefit of the remedies attached to the kind of contract they had wanted to enter into. In other words, the contemporary concept of consensualism or freedom of contract, in the sense that any agreement willingly and freely entered into, and not in violation of public order, can be binding on the parties, was un-

---

4. Black's Law Dictionary (7th ed): *emptio* [Latin "purchase"], Roman and Civil Law. The act of buying: a purchase … *Emptio et venditio* [Latin: "purchase and sell"]: caveat emptor [Latin: "let the buyer beware"].

5. See, for example, the methodical structure of civil law Codes.

6. Justinian (note 1 supra): Lib.III, Tit. XV.

7. Id. Lib.III. Tit. XVI.

8. Id. Lib. III. Tit.XXIII.

known in Roman law. There existed a series of 'contracts' but no single concept of "contract."[9]

In contemporary civil law jurisdictions, we still find these general kinds of contracts elaborated by the Roman jurists and within each kind there exist special nominate contracts[10] as was the case also in Roman law. Among the *real contracts*, we find, for example:

Mutuum, or Loan for Consumption: at Roman law: Inst. III 15; Fr. Civ. C. Arts 1892, 1893; La Civ. C. Arts 2910, 2911; German Civ. C., BGB Art. 607[11].

If we turn to *consensual contracts*, we can refer to the contract of sale of movable things in particular:

Roman law Inst. III. XXII; Fr Civ. C. Art. 1598: La Civ.C. Art. 2458; BGB Art. 433.

Another very interesting classification of contracts found in contemporary civil law systems can be traced back to Roman law. The common law, on the other hand, has taken a very different path. The classification we want to point to here very briefly is between unilateral contracts and bilateral contracts[12].

A unilateral contract was, at Roman law, a contract that created an obligation or duty on one party only, and a right or benefit in the other party. Conversely, a bilateral contract created obligations on both sides of the contractual relationship and, necessarily, vested rights of action on both sides also. Turning to contemporary civil law and civil Codes we find the following definitions:

Fr. Civ. C.

Art. 1103: It is *unilateral* where one or more persons are bound towards one or several others, without there being any obligation on the part of the latter.

Art. 1104: It is *commutative* where each party binds himself to transfer or do a thing which is considered as the equivalent of what is transferred to

---

9. It is interesting to point out here the similarity of the Roman law of "contracts" and the English common law of "contracts" before Roman law would., later on, evolve in the Middle Ages.

10. "Nominate" because they have been given a name in a civil Code: ex, Sale, Deposit, Lease....

11. For the common law, see, for example, State v. Brown, 102 SW 394, 1907.

12. For details, see below p.28 et seq.

him or of what is done for him. (project of new law of obligations: Art. 1102-1)

La. Civ. C.

Art. 1907: A contract is unilateral when the party who accepts the obligation of the other does not assume a reciprocal obligation.

Art. 1908: A contract is bilateral, or synallagmatic, when the parties obligate themselves reciprocally, so that the obligation of each party is correlative to the obligation of the other.

BGB

§ 111: Unilateral legal transactions

A unilateral legal transaction that the minor enters into without the necessary consent of the legal representative is ineffective. If the minor enters into such a legal transaction with another person with this consent, the legal transaction is ineffective if the minor does not produce the consent in writing and the other person without undue delay rejects the legal transaction for this reason. Rejection is not possible if the representative had given the other person notice of the consent.

§ 241: (1) By virtue of the obligation the obligee is entitled to demand performance from the obligor. The performance may also consist of an omission.

(2) The obligation may also, depending on its concerns, oblige each party to take account of the rights, legally protected interests and other interests of the other party.

At common law, the notions of unilateral and bilateral contract are quite different from their civil law "synonyms," also "faux-amis"!. Whereas at civil law *unilateral* and *bilateral* refer to the existence or not of 'reciprocal' obligations,[13] at common law the same adjectives *unilateral* and *bilateral* have to do with the manifestation of one will (unilateral) or two wills (bilateral). In other words, at civil law the same two adjectives are concerned with the per-formance of existing obligations whereas at common law the two adjectives have to do with the formation of the contract.[14]

---

13. "Unilateral," somewhat like a 'one-way street'; "bilateral," somewhat like a 'two-way street.'

14. See more below p.39–122. See also, Le contrat en droit américain, by Alain A. Levasseur, Dalloz Connaissance du Droit, p.15–16, 1996.

B. Historical Survey of Contract at Civil Law and Contracts at Common Law

1. Civil Law

The concept of *consensualism* was originally unknown at Roman law. Although consent (*cum sentire*) was a component element of a contract, it was not sufficient, by itself, to create a contract. A material, physical, or formal element mostly, was required for a contract to be created. Formalism, under one form or another, in a sense was prevailing as it included also an element of proof.

Consent came to be considered essential and sufficient in some contracts as a result of the need to adapt to the expediency of commercial transactions and to facilitate these transactions by relying on the parties' exchange of consent and good faith. In answer to these commercial needs, the contracts of sale, lease, mandate ... would become merely consensual contracts. They were binding as a result of the exchange of consent between the parties, in addition to each contract meeting the proper requirements of its own legal identity, such as a price and a thing in a contract of sale, a thing for a thing in a contract of exchange.... Although 'consent' made some inroads into the prevailing principle of 'formalism,' the latter continued to govern the law of contract in the civil law system until it was confronted with canon law in the Middle Ages. Canon law was based on the moral foundation that promises between men are binding because of the good faith,[15] *fides*, that must exist in a relationship of trust. To breach a promise was to breach that *fides* and to be guilty of a lie. Canon law was, therefore, diametrically opposed to the formalism of Roman law. But the canon law lawyers realized quickly how dangerous and threatening a *nuda promissio*, a bare promise, could be if not subject to some control. So the canon lawyers gave in to the civil lawyers on this issue of consent and the focus was then placed on *cause* or reason, hence a subjective concept, as another requirement for a binding contract. This emphasis of the canonists on the *cause* of a contract at civil law will explain, to a large extent, why, in turn, the common law will require a *consideration*, as a form of "objective cause," for a contract to be binding.[16]

---

15. On good faith, see below p.99–122.
16. On cause and consideration, see below p.79–98.

In the 13th century, the principle of consensualism will begin to make some inroads into the growing influence of customary law. Next to the "oath" which was the traditional means of making a contract binding, customary law introduced a simpler means of binding parties to their contract: the propriety, the accepted standard of behavior. There developed the concept of *pacta sunt servanda* meaning that an agreement must be respected because "it is the proper, expected, thing to do." Loysel was to express this binding force of contract as follows: *oxen are bound by their horns, men by their words.*[17]

Nowadays, the civil Codes governing many civil law jurisdictions have adopted, as the dominant principle, the principle of consensualism in their law of contract. Formalism is also recognized as a principle for very specific reasons, such as that of the proof of the seriousness of a deal, or the intended protection of a particular party. Still, formalism is secondary to the principle of consensualism.[18]

2. Common Law

The history of the English common law of contracts is closely tied to the history of the writ system in English law. Four writs, or rights of action,

---

17. Institutes Coutumières, Liv. III Tit.1 art.2, "*On lie les boeufs par les cornes, et les hommes par les paroles; et autant vaut une simple promesse ou convenance, que les stipulations du droit romain.*"

18. Fr. Civ. C. Art. 1108: Four requirements are essential for the validity of a convention:
    -consent of the party who binds herself;
    -capacity to contract;
    -an object which is the matter of the commitment;
    -a cause which justifies the commitment";

La. Civ. C. Art. 1927: A contract is formed by the consent of the parties established through offer and acceptance. Unless the law prescribes a certain formality for the intended contract, offer and acceptance may be made orally, in writing, or by action or inaction that under the circumstances is clearly indicative of consent. Unless otherwise specified in the offer, there need not be conformity between the manner in which the offer is made and the manner in which the acceptance is made.; BGB § 145: Any person who offers to another to enter into a contract is bound by the offer, unless he has excluded being bound by it." BGB § 151: A contract comes into existence through the acceptance of the offer without the offeror needing to be notified of acceptance, if such a declaration is not to be expected according to common usage, or if the offeror has waved it. The moment when the offer expires is determined according to the intention of the offeror which is to be inferred from the offer or the circumstances.

which gave access to the royal courts concerned relationships which can be identified today with contracts: they were the *writ of debt* (whereby the defendant was ordered to pay back to the plaintiff a sum of money for whatever reason), the *writ of detinue* (in the situation where the defendant was 'withholding' something against the will of the plaintiff), the *writ of trespass* (where an unlawful act had been committed against a person or a person's property) and the *writ of covenant* (an action available to recover for non performance of a promise made under seal). None of these actions or writs could entitle a plaintiff to seek the performance of a consensual obligation.[19]

It is mostly in the XVth century that the common law of contract began to assume its identity. Out of the action of trespass, which was available in those instances where there had been a direct and unauthorized damage caused to a person or a thing, what we would call a tort today, grew the actions on the case. The first one created was in the event the defendant had been guilty of misfeasance. The second one was created later in those instances where it could be found that the defendant had been guilty of nonfeasance. The third step occurred with the coming into existence of the action of *assumpsit* (from the latin *assumere*, assumption) grounded on the 'assumption' that the defendant had undertaken to carry out some commitment which he performed poorly thereby causing a prejudice to the plaintiff. Subsequently, the action of *assumpsit* was extended to those instances where, instead of poorly performing his duty, the defendant had not performed his duty and, thereby, had caused a prejudice to the plaintiff.

Despite the existence of these two forms of *assumpsit*, or special *assumpsit*, it remained that the plaintiff still had to establish that some form of tort had been committed by the defendant who had bound himself to carry out a duty and either failed to carry out that duty or carried it out poorly and, in both instances, had caused a prejudice to the defendant. It remained that consent alone, without a commitment to carryout a duty, was not sufficient to justify the existence of a right of action. One reason was, in the XVth century, that formalism permeated all aspects of the law and another reason was the existence, still today, of the writ of debt. The common law judges, or judges of the common law courts, to contain the extension of their jurisdiction by the judges of the Chancery Court or Court of Equity, made a further step forward when, by inductive reasoning, they stated that behind the non

---

19. At common law "obligation" has a different meaning from the meaning it had at civil law; at common law it meant 'duty' owed; at civil law it meant 'bond of law,' *vinculum juris*.

performance of a consensual promise it was possible to assert that there existed a prejudice suffered by a plaintiff who expected and relied on the performance of his promise by the defendant-debtor. The <u>non</u> performance of the promise was tantamount to a <u>poor</u> performance of that promise. The courts defined the overall framework of the action by requiring that either there should exist a breach of performance of a bargain, in the sense of a reciprocal agreement between the parties, or that if one party had made a promise to another party the latter had relied on that promise with the consequence that she suffered a prejudice when the promise had not been carried out. However, a purely <u>moral</u> obligation could not give rise to a right of action because there was no bargain between the parties or no possible material loss had been suffered by either one. The concept of consideration was born.[20]

Slade's Case[21]

Trin. 44 Eliz. In the King's Bench

John Slade brought an action on the case in the King's Bench against Humphrey Morley,[...] and declared, that whereas the plaintiff, 10th of November, 36 Eliz. was possessed of a close of land in Halberton, [...] containing by estimation eight acres for the term of divers years then and yet to come, and being so possessed, the plaintiff the said 10th day of November, the said close has sowed with wheat and rye, which wheat and rye, 8 Maii, 37 Eliz. were grown into blades, the defendant, in consideration that the plaintiff, at the special insistence and request of the said Humphrey, had bargained and sold to him the said blades of wheat and rye growing upon the said close (A),[...] assumed and promised the plaintiff to pay him 16l. at the Feast of St. John the Baptist then to come: and for non-payment thereof at the said Feast of St. John the Baptist, the plaintiff brought the said action:[...] the jurors gave a special verdict, *sc.* that the defendant bought of the plaintiff the wheat and rye in blades growing upon the said close as is aforesaid, *prout* in the said declaration is alleged, and further found, that between the plaintiff and the defendant there was no other promise or assumption but only the said bargain; and against the maintenance of this action divers objections were made[...] 1. That the plaintiff upon this bargain might have ordinary remedy by action of debt, which is an action formed in

---

20. Subsequently the action of *assumpsit* will be extended to instances of *quantum meruit* and *quantum valebat/valebant.*

21. 4 Co. REP. 92b (1602), 76 ER 1074.

the register, and therefore he should not have an action on the case, which is an extraordinary action[...]. The second objection was, that the maintenance of this action takes away the defendant's benefit of (*a*) wager of law, and so bereaves him of the benefit which the law gives him, which is his birthright[...].

It was resolved, that every contract (*b*) executory imports in itself an *assumpsit*, for when one agrees to pay money, or to deliver any thing, thereby he assumes or promises to pay, or deliver it, and therefore when one sells any goods to another, and agrees to deliver them at a day to come, and the other in consideration thereof agrees to pay so much money as such a day, in that case both parties may have an action of debt, or an action on the case of *assumpsit*, for the mutual executory agreement of both parties imports in itself reciprocal actions upon the case, as well as actions of debt[...]

Chapter Two

Juridical Acts and Contracts

A. Juridical Acts

Many civil law jurisdictions make a distinction between juridical acts and juridical facts. This distinction, made on the basis of the source of an obligation, has been elaborated mostly by civil law scholars, or doctrine. It can be found today in the civil Code of Québec[3] and the Projet Catala[4] which proposes substantial revisions to the articles of the French Civil Code on the law of Obligations and Prescription.

This classification and division of all types of bonds of law into 'juridical acts' and 'juridical facts' is very illustrative of the inductive and deductive methods of reasoning at civil law. The essence of the difference between juridical acts and juridical facts consists in the following: a juridical act is the expression of a person's will manifested with the intention to create specific legal effects by entering willingly into a bond of law; on the other hand, a juridical fact is an event, devoid of human will, which, when it occurs, brings about the existence of an obligation creative of legal effects. A typical illustration of a juridical act is a "contract" whereby a party, the obligor, may bind himself/herself to give, to do or not to do something for the bene-

---

3. Civil Code of Québec: Article 1371: It is of the essence of an obligation that there be persons between whom it exists, a prestation which forms its object, and, in the case of an obligation arising out of a juridical act, a cause which justifies its existence; Article 1372: An obligation arises from a contract or from any act or fact to which the effects of an obligation are attached by law.

4. Avant-Projet de Réforme du Droit des Obligations et du Droit de la Prescription, Pierre Catala, 22 septembre 2005; see French Ministry of Justice website and Association Henri Capitant website. See: Article 1105-1 : The offer is a unilateral act that identifies the essential elements of the contract ... expressing the will of the offeror to be bound should the offer be accepted; Article 1105-5: Acceptance is a unilateral act whereby its author states his will to be bound by the stipulations of the offer. [translation into English by A. Levasseur and D. Gruning: see Association Henri Capitant website].

fit of the other party to the contract. A tort, or delict in civil law terms, would be an example of a juridical fact. Should an accident occur, as a consequence of the accident, the tortfeasor-obligor will have to pay damages to the victim-obligee.

Let us further illustrate this distinction with some details. A juridical act being the manifestation of the will, that will could be expressed by one person only; in this instance the single will gives rise to a *unilateral juridical act;* a testament or "last will" and the acknowledgment of a child are two examples of unilateral juridical acts.[5] On the other hand, a juridical act could be created by an exchange of 'wills' expressed by two persons; this exchange of wills carries with it the creation of a *bilateral juridical act.* For example, in a contract of sale the seller sells something which must be delivered to a buyer who, in return, must pay the price to the seller. If more than two parties, i.e. multiple parties, are expressing their wills with the intent to be bound to perform obligations, the juridical act could be referred to as *'collective'* (ex: collective agreements). Regardless of the adjective which may precede the words 'juridical act,' the focus of the analysis must be placed on the 'will' which must meet some specific criteria if it is meant to create legal effects on a person, for a person or between persons. We will look, below, at some selected criteria which will be the intent or will of parties and the cause-consideration necessary for a contract to be binding between the parties to it[6].

The common law does not know this concept of 'juridical act.' Actually, broadly speaking, the common law does not concern itself with many abstractions or concepts. The pragmatism of the common law, its historical development and the role of juries can explain this lack of concern for abstractions. Whereas the growth and originality of the civil law are mostly the work of doctrinal writers who can be theoretical in their legal thinking, the common law has been much more the creation of the courts and case-law which have to be more practical and relational in addressing and solving legal issues.

Although, at common law, the 'wills' of two parties are necessary for a contract to exist, as such the 'will' is not sufficient to bind the parties. At civil law, on the other hand, a party can bind herself by a juridical act by the mere

---

5. La. Civ. C. Art. 1575: "A. An olographic testament is one entirely written, dated, and signed in the handwriting of the testator ..." Art. 196: "A man may, by authentic act or by signing the birth certificate, acknowledge a child not filiated to another man ...".

6. On intent, will, see below p. 39–77; on cause-consideration, see below p. 79–98.

authority attached to her 'will.' Let us consider, as illustrations, the following definitions or descriptions of what amounts to a 'contract.'

B. Notion of "Contract" at Civil Law

Roman Law

Institutes of Justinian, Book III, Title XXII "De Consensu Obligatione"[7]:

Obligations are formed by the mere consent of the parties in the contracts of sale … An obligation is, in these cases, said to be made by the mere consent of the parties, because there is no necessity for any writing, not even for the presence of the parties ;nor is it requisite that anything should be given to make the contract binding, but the mere consent of those between whom the transaction is carried on suffices....

BGB

§ 145: "Any person who offers to another to enter into a contract is bound by the offer, unless he has excluded being bound by it."

§ 146: "An offer expires if it is refused as against the offeror, or if it is not accepted as against this person in due time in accordance with Sections 147 to 149."

Fr. Civ. C

Article 1101: "A contract is a convention whereby one or more parties bind themselves towards one or more other parties, to give, to do or not to do something."

Article 1134 § 1: "Conventions legally entered into have the effect of law for the parties …"

La. Civ. C.

Article 1906: "A contract is an agreement by two or more parties whereby obligations are created, modified, or extinguished."

---

7. Introduction to the American Edition of Sandars' Institutes of Justinian, by William G. Hammon, LL.D. 1876.

Article 1927: "A contract is formed by the consent of the parties established through offer and acceptance.

Unless the law prescribes a certain formality for the intended contract, offer and acceptance may be made orally, in writing, or by action or inaction that under the circumstances is clearly indicative of consent."

Sw. Fed. C.O.

Article 1: "A contract requires the mutual agreement of the parties. This agreement may be either express or implied."

C.C.Q.

Article 1378 : "A contract is an agreement of wills by which one or several persons oblige themselves to one or several other persons to perform a prestation...."

C. Notion of "Contract" at Common Law

English Common Law
William Blackstone: Commentaries on the Laws of England
(1765–1769) by George Sharswood, 1860.

Book II. Ch.XXX. Of Title by Gift, Grant, and Contract.

IX. A contract, which usually conveys an interest merely in action, is thus defined: " an agreement, upon sufficient consideration, to do or not to do a particular thing." From which definition there arise three points to be contemplated in all contracts; 1.The *agreement*: 2. The *consideration*: and 3. The *thing* to be done or omitted, or the different species of contracts.

First then it is an *agreement*, a mutual bargain or convention; and therefore there must at least be two contracting parties of sufficient ability to make a contract; ...

Lord Diplock

"The law of contract is part of the law of obligations. The English law of obligations is about their sources and the remedies.... English law is thus concerned with contracts as a source of obligations. The basic principle which the law of contract seeks to enforce is that a person who makes a promise to another ought to keep his promise. This basic principle is subject to an historical exception that English law does not give the promisee a remedy for the failure by a promisor to perform his promise unless either the promise was made in a particular form, e.g. under seal, or the promisee in return promises to do something for the promisor, which he would not otherwise be obliged to do, i.e. gives consideration for the promise.... Each promise that a promisor makes to a promisee by entering into a contract with him creates an obligation to perform it owed by the promisor as obligor to the promisee as obligee ..."[8]

G.H. Treitel, Q.C., The Law of Contract
Seventh Edition, Stevens & Sons, 1987.

"A contract is an agreement giving rise to obligations which are enforced or recognized by law. The factor which distinguishes contractual from other legal obligations is that they are based on the agreement of the contracting parties ... [...] the law of contract is concerned with the circumstances in which agreements are legally binding..[...] The bulk of the law of contract is concerned with the questions of agreement and legal enforceability;..[...]the agreement of the parties is irrelevant to the question whether a contract is to be enforced specifically, or only by an award of damages. But the agreement between the parties may be relevant in determining the precise amount of damages which will be awarded for a breach of contract ...

An agreement is made when one party accepts an offer made by the other. Further requirements are that the agreement must be certain and final; ..."[9]

United States Law
Restatement, 2d

§ 1. Contract Defined.

A contract is a promise or a set of promises for the breach of which the law gives a remedy, or the performance of which the law in some way recognizes as a duty."

---

8. In Lep Air Services v. Rolloswin Ltd, House of Lords [1973] AC 331 at p.346–347.
9. G.H. Treitel p.1–7.

§ 3. Agreement Defined; Bargain Defined.

An agreement is a manifestation of mutual assent on the part of two or more persons. A bargain is an agreement to exchange promises or to exchange a promise for a performance or to exchange performances.

UCC

§ 1-201 (3): "Agreement," as distinguished from "contract," means the bargain of the parties in fact, as found in their language or inferred from other circumstances, including course of performance, course of dealing, or usage of trade as provided in Section 1-303

§ 1-201 (12): "Contract," as distinguished from "agreement," means the total legal obligation that results from the parties' agreement as determined by [the Uniform Commercial Code] as supplemented by any other applicable laws.

E. Allan Farnsworth: Contracts
Fourth Edition, Aspen, 2004

A. THE MEANING AND ROLE OF CONTRACT

§ 1.1. The Meaning of *Contract.* [there are] two limitations on the scope of the law of contracts. The first limitation is that the law of contracts is confined to promises that the law will *enforce....* The second limitation ... is that the law of contracts is confined to *promises.* It is therefore concerned with exchanges that relate to the *future* because a "promise" is a commitment as to future behavior ...

D. International/Multinational

UNIDROIT

Article 2.1.1 : "A contract may be concluded either by the acceptance of an offer or by conduct of the parties that is sufficient to show agreement"

Article 3.2: "A contract is concluded, modified or terminated by the mere agreement of the parties, without any further requirement."

CISG

Article 4 : "This Convention governs only the formation of the contract of sale..... .[I]t is not concerned with: (a) the validity of the contract...."

Article 23: "A contract is concluded at the moment when an acceptance of an offer becomes effective ...

Article 29 (1) A contract may be modified or terminated by the mere agreement of the parties.

Principles of European Contract Law, Parts I and II
Edited by Ole Lando and Hugh Beale
Kluwer Law International, 2000
The Commission on European Contract Law

Section 1: General Provisions

Article 2:101: Conditions for the conclusion of a contract

(1) A contract is concluded if:

(a) the parties intend to be legally bound, and

(b) they reach a sufficient agreement without any further requirement.

(2) A contract need not be concluded or evidenced in writing nor is it subject to any other requirements as to form. The contract may be proved by any means, including witnesses.

Article 2:103: Sufficient Agreement

(1) There is sufficient agreement if the terms:

(a) have been sufficiently defined by the parties so that the contract can be enforced, or

(b) can be determined under these Principles.

(2) However, if one of the parties refuses to conclude a contract unless the parties have agreed on some specific matter, there is no contract unless agreement on that matter has been reached.

E. Courts' Decisions

1. Civil Law Courts

Fr. Cour de cassation
Cass. civ. 10 oct.1995, Bull. civ. I No 352.

On Jan. 8,1991, M.Frata won a substantial amount of money at the horse-track. The winning combination was on the "Quinté plus." M. d'Onofrio stated, that M. Frata, together with some colleagues, would normally entrust him with the responsibility of having the "Quinté" tickets validated by the PMU; he stated also that it had been agreed that he, d'Onofrio, would receive 10% of the winnings; that on this last race, he could not enter the ticket received from Frata and, thus, personally re-wrote the ticket and switched around the numbers previously selected by Frata; that Frata had the winning ticket on the race and that, after the race, Frata promised d'Onofrio that he would receive his share of the proceeds, but that Frata, eventually, refused to carry out his promise. D'Onofrio is seeking payment of "his" 10%.

The Court: ... M.Frata argued that his promise carried no civil consequences ... ; Whereas, the transformation — improperly qualified as a novation — of a natural obligation into a civil obligation, which is grounded in a unilateral commitment to carry out a natural obligation, does not require that a civil obligation be in existence before that natural obligation,..;

[The civil Chamber of the Cour de Cassation ruled that the Court of Appeal rightfully held that M.Frata had meant to transform his natural obligation into a civil obligation]

Cour du Québec: Construction Polaris Inc. c. Conseil de bande Micmacs de Gesgapegiag

J.E. 97-1341 (C.Q.)

Juge Denis Robert :

[...]

3 According to the principles stated in articles 1378 et seq. of the Civil Code of Québec, one must not mix up a contract with the writing which incorporate its wording; the contract is the agreement between the parties and the writing is merely a means of proving the existence of the contract.

5 The acceptance by the defendants represents that moment when the contract was formed, ...

6 a. Art.1387: The contract is formed at that moment when the offeror receives the acceptance and where the acceptance is received, regardless of the method of communication used ...

2. Common Law Courts

U.K.

Rann and Other Executors of Mary Hughes v. Isabella Hughes, Administratrix of J. Hughes in Error
[cited in Mitchinson v. Hewson 7 T. R. 350]

[...]

"It is undoubtedly true that every man is by the law of nature, bound to ful-fil his engagements. It is equally true that the law of this country supplies no means, nor affords any remedy, to compel the performance of an agreement made without sufficient consideration; such agreement is nudum pactum ex quo non oritur action; and whatsoever may be the sense of this maxim in the civil law, it is in the last-mentioned sense only that it is to be understood in our law. [...] if I promise generally to pay upon request what I was li-able to pay upon request in another right, I derive no advantage or conven-ience from this promise, and therefore there is not sufficient consideration for it. But it is said that if this promise is in writing that takes away the ne-cessity of a consideration, and obviates the objection of nudum pactum, for that cannot be where the promise is put in writing[...] that there cannot be nudum pactum in writing whatever may be the rule of the civil law, there is certainly none such in the law of England. [...] All contracts are, by the laws of England, distinguished into agreements by specialty, and agree-ments by parol; nor is there any such third class as some of the counsel have endeavoured to maintain, as contracts in writing. If they be merely written and not specialties, they are parol, and a consideration must be proved."

Rose and Frank Company v. J.R. Crompton and Brothers, Limited, and Others
[1923] 2 K.B. 261

[...] The document, after purporting to set out the understanding between the parties, including several modifications of their previous arrangement, pro-ceeded in these words: "This arrangement is not entered into, nor is this mem-orandum written, as a formal or legal agreement, and shall not be subject to legal jurisdiction in the law courts either in the United States or England, but it is only a definite expression and record of the purpose and intention of the three parties concerned to which they each honourably pledge themselves with the fullest confidence, based on past business with each other, that it will be carried through by each of the three parties with mutual loyalty and friendly cooperation."[...] the American firm brought an action for breach of the contract[...]

SCRUTTON L.J. [...] Now it is quite possible for parties to come to an agreement by accepting a proposal with the result that the agreement concluded does not give rise to legal relations. The reason of this is that the parties do not intend that their agreement shall give rise to legal relations. This intention may be implied from the subject matter of the agreement, but it may also be expressed by the parties. In social and family relations such an intention is readily implied, while in business matters the opposite result would ordinarily follow. But I can see no reason why, even in business matters, the parties should not intend to rely on each other's good faith and honour, and to exclude all idea of settling disputes by any outside intervention, with the accompanying necessity of expressing themselves so precisely that outsiders may have no difficulty in understanding what they mean. If they clearly express such an intention I can see no reason in public policy why effect should not be given to their intention. [...] I come to the [...] conclusion[...], that the particular clause in question shows a clear intention by the parties that the rest of their arrangement or agreement shall not affect their legal relations, or be enforceable in a Court of law. [...]

ATKIN L.J. [...] To create a contract there must be a common intention of the parties to enter into legal obligations, mutually communicated expressly or impliedly. Such an intention ordinarily will be inferred when parties enter into an agreement which in other respects conforms to the rules of law as to the formation of contracts. It may be negatived impliedly by the nature of the agreed promise or promises, as in the case of offer and acceptance of hospitality, or of some agreements made in the course of family life between members of a family [...] In this document, construed as a whole, I find myself driven to the conclusion that the clause in question expresses in clear terms the mutual intention of the parties not to enter into legal obligations in respect to the matters upon which they are recording their agreement. I have never seen such a clause before, but I see nothing necessarily absurd in business men seeking to regulate their business relations by mutual promises which fall short of legal obligations, and rest on obligations of either honour or self-interest, or perhaps both. In this agreement I consider the clause a dominant clause, and not to be rejected, as the learned judge thought, on the ground of repugnancy.[...]

Jones v. Padavatton
[1969] 2 All E.R. 616

[Facts: The daughter of a resident in Trinidad was employed[...]at the Indian embassy in Washington in the United States. Although she said she was unwilling to leave, she accepted an offer made by her mother in august 1962 that if she would go to England and read for the Bar with a view to practicing as a lawyer in Trinidad, the mother would provide maintenance for her at the rate of $200 a month [...] equivalent to £42 a month.[...] The daughter went to England in November 1962 and entered on her studies at the Bar, her fees and maintenance at the offered rate being paid by her mother. But no terms of the arrangements were recorded in writing and no statement of the parties' respective obligations and in particular nothing as to the duration of the arrangement. [...] a proposal was made by the mother in 1964 that she should buy a house of some size in London in a room or rooms of which the daughter could reside with her son(she was divorced from her husband) the rents from letting other rooms furnished to provide maintenance in place of the £42 a month. A house was bought for £6,000 and conveyed to the mother, who provided the money in several sums though not all that for incidental expenses and furniture. The daughter [...] moved in during January 1965, tenants beginning to arrive in the next month. Again there was no written arrangement and incidental matters remained unsettled [...] No money from the rents was received by the mother, nor was she supplied with any accounts. In 1967 the mother issued a summons claiming possession of the house from the daughter, who counterclaimed for to £1,655 18s. 9d. said to have been paid in respect of the house. At the hearing some of Part I of the Bar examination remained to be taken by the daughter and also the whole of Part 2 (the final).]

SALMON, L.J.: [...] The first point to be decided is whether or not there was ever a legally binding agreement between the mother and the daughter in relation to the daughter's reading for the Bar in England. [...]

Did the parties intend the arrangement to be legally binding? This question has to be solved by applying what is sometimes (although perhaps unfortunately) called an objective test. The court has to consider what the parties said and wrote in the light of all the surrounding circumstances, and then decide whether the true inference is that the ordinary man and woman, speaking or writing thus in such circumstances, would have intended to create a legally binding agreement.[...]

In the present case the learned county court judge, having had the advantage of seeing the mother and the daughter in the witness box, entirely accepted the daughter's version of the facts. He came to the conclusion [...] that the arrangement between the parties prior to the daughter's leaving Washington were intended by both to have contractual force. [...] The mother [...] eventually persuaded the daughter to do as she wished by promising her that, if she threw up her excellent position in Washington and came to study for the Bar in England, she would pay her daughter an allowance of $200 a month until she had completed her studies. [...] I cannot think that either intended that if, after the daughter had been in London, say, for six months, the mother dishonoured her promise and left her daughter destitute, the daughter would have no legal redress.

In the very special circumstances of this case, I consider that the true inference must be that neither the mother nor the daughter could have intended that the daughter should have no legal right to receive, and the mother no legal obligation to pay, the allowance of $200 a month.[...]

The evidence shows that all the arrangements in relation to the house were very vague and made without any contractual intent. By this arrangement the mother was trying primarily to help the daughter, and also perhaps to make a reasonable investment for herself[...] Nothing was said as to how much the daughter might pay herself out of the rents for maintenance. [...] She seems to take the view (as does the learned county court judge) that she has a legal claim on the mother to house her and contribute to her support and that of her son and husband, perhaps in perpetuity. In this she is mistaken, and so in my judgment is the learned county court judge. The mother began this action for possession[...] in 1967. For the reasons I have indicated, there is in my view no defence to the action, and I would accordingly allow the appeal.[...]

U.S.A.

W.O. Lucy and J.C. Lucy v. A.H. Zehmer and Ida S. Zehmer

[196 Va. 493, 84 S.E. 2d 516, 1954]

BUCHANAN, J., delivered the opinion of the court.

[...].

The instrument sought to be enforced was written by A.H. Zehmer on December 20, 1952, in these words: 'We hereby agree to sell to W.O. Lucy the Ferguson Farm complete for $50,000.00, title satisfactory to buyer,' and signed by the defendants, A.H. Zehmer and Ida S. Zehmer.

The answer of A.H. Zehmer admitted that at the time mentioned W.O. Lucy offered him $50,000 cash for the farm, but that he, Zehmer, considered that the offer was made in jest; that so thinking, and both he and Lucy having had several drinks, he wrote out 'the memorandum' quoted above and induced his wife to sign it; that he did not deliver the memorandum to Lucy, but that Lucy picked it up, read it, put it in his pocket, attempted to offer Zehmer $5 to bind the bargain, which Zehmer refused to accept, and realizing for the first time that Lucy was serious, Zehmer assured him that he had no intention of selling the farm and that the whole matter was a joke. Lucy left the premises insisting that he had purchased the farm.[...]

The mental assent of the parties is not requisite for the formation of a contract. If the words or other acts of one of the parties have but one reasonable meaning, his undisclosed intention is immaterial except when an unreasonable meaning which he attaches to his manifestations is known to the other party. [...]

An agreement or mutual assent is of course essential to a valid contract but the law imputes to a person an intention corresponding to the reasonable meaning of his words and acts. [...]

So a person cannot set up that he was merely jesting when his conduct and words would warrant a reasonable person in believing that he intended a real agreement [...]

Specific performance, it is true, is not a matter of absolute or arbitrary right, but is addressed to the reasonable and sound discretion of the court[...] But it is likewise true that the discretion which may be exercised is not an arbitrary or capricious one, but one which is controlled by the established doctrines and settled principles of equity; and, generally, where a contract is in its nature and circumstances unobjectionable, it is as much a matter of course for courts of equity to decree a specific performance of it as it is for a court of law to give damages for a breach of it.

The complainants are entitled to have specific performance of the contracts sued on. [...]

Morris Lefkowitz v. Great Minneapolis Surplus Store, Inc.
[251 Minn. 188, 86 N.W. 2d 689, 1957]

MURPHY, Justice.

[...]

The defendant contends that a newspaper advertisement offering items of merchandise for sale at a named price is a 'unilateral offer' which may be withdrawn without notice [...] Such advertisements have been construed as an invitation for an offer of sale on the terms stated, which offer, when received, may be accepted or rejected and which therefore does not become a contract of sale until accepted by the seller; and until a contract has been so made, the seller may modify or revoke such prices or terms.[...]

There are numerous authorities which hold that a particular advertisement in a newspaper or circular letter relating to a sale of articles may be construed by the court as constituting an offer, acceptance of which would complete a contract.[...]

The test of whether a binding obligation may originate in advertisements addressed to the general public is 'whether the facts show that some performance was promised in positive terms in return for something requested.' [...]

We are of the view on the facts before us that the offer by the defendant of the sale of the Lapin fur was clear, definite, and explicit, and left nothing open for negotiation. The plaintiff having successful managed to be the first one to appear at the seller's place of business to be served, as requested by the advertisement, and having offered the stated purchase price of the article, he was entitled to performance on the part of the defendant. [...]while an advertiser has the right at any time before acceptance to modify his offer, he does not have the right, after acceptance, to impose new or arbitrary conditions not contained in the published offer.

Chapter Three

Types of Contracts

The Civil Law and the Common Law Contrasted

The adjectives selected below [bilateral, unilateral, onerous, gratuitous] "qualify" or "identify" four different types of contracts in the civil law systems and, thus, provide us with an opportunity to illustrate a fundamental feature of the civil law legal methodology and culture which is to describe and place legal relations into self contained "legal categories." Civilians are 'culturally' inclined to "categorize" which is a function "crucial to [the civilian] perceptions and understanding of data, and the categories [civilians] erect result from [their] experience and in turn affect [their] perceptions and, therefore, [their] experiences."[10] The common law itself is not a total stranger to this process of classification as illustrated by E.A. Farnsworth and G.H. Treitel in the excerpts below.[11]

To submit a legal relationship which is made up of several component parts to this process of categorization or classification amounts, actually, to fitting this relationship into a pre-set legal order or legal framework, made up of well identified legal rules. It is to devise a particular legal regime for each classified type of relationship. Thus, within one legal category or legal institution will be included a multiplicity of factual relationships bound together by a common core of well established and necessary component legal bonds which are built into a legal regime by a reasoning process which starts from the particular to rise, by inductive reasoning, to the general.

The four categories of contracts we are presenting here are good illustrations of this process of categorization or classification. But they are much more. Indeed, in this selective analysis of contracts in comparative law, "we cannot restrict ourselves to the literal translation of texts; for we want more

---

10. Vivian Grosswald Curran, Comparative Law, An Introduction, Carolina Academic Press, 2002, p.48.

11. See next page.

than textual knowledge; we want effective, practical knowledge of the conceptual horizon.... We must allow the concepts of the foreign law to become images and then describe them in our language ..." Furthermore, "we ... must separate languages that privilege the abstract expression from those that emphasize the concrete." We believe that this topical comparison between fundamentally different concepts of contracts that bear the same names in the civil law and the common law will turn our fixation on "words" into concepts shaped and chiseled by our own cultural "images."[12]

A: Bilateral Contracts and Unilateral Contracts

1. At Civil Law

a: Concepts

Fr. Civ. C.

Art. 1102: A contract is synallagmatic or bilateral when the parties obligate themselves reciprocally towards each other.

Art. 1103: It is unilateral when one or more parties are bound towards one or more parties without any reciprocal obligation on the part of the latter parties.

La. Civ. C.

Art. 1907: A contract is unilateral when the party who accepts the obligation of the other does not assume a reciprocal obligation.

Art. 1908: A contract is bilateral, or synallagmatic, when the parties obligate themselves reciprocally, so that the obligation of each party is correlative to the obligation of the other.

C.C.Q.

Art. 1380: A contract is synallagmatic, or bilateral when the parties obligate themselves reciprocally, each to the other, so that the obligation of one party is correlative to the obligation of the other.

When one party obligates himself to the other without any obligation on the part of the latter, the contract is unilateral.

---

12. Vivian G. Curran, supra, p.32–37.

Sw. Fed. C.O.

Art. 82: The party who demands performance of a bilateral contract by the other must either....

Art. 107: Where in the case of bilateral contracts a debtor is in default ...

b: Illustrations

b-1: Bilateral or synallagmatic contracts

Sw. Fed. C.O.

Art. 237: The contract of exchange is governed by the law of sales in the sense that each of the contracting parties is considered seller as to the goods promised to the other party and buyer as to the goods promised by the other party.

La. Civ. C.

Art. 2439: Sale is a contract whereby a person transfers ownership of a thing to another for a price in money. The thing, the price, and the consent of the parties are requirements for the perfection of a sale.

C.C.Q.

Art. 1851: Lease is a contract by which a person, the lessor, undertakes to provide another person, the lessee, in return for a rent, with the enjoyment of a movable or immovable property for a certain time.

b-2: Unilateral contracts

Sw. Fed. C.O.

Art. 239: A gift means any transfer *inter vivos* whereby a person gives to another all or part of his property without receiving a corresponding consideration ...

It. Civ. C.

Art. 1331: Option. When the parties agree that one of them is to remain bound by his declaration and that the other has the power to accept or not, the declaration of the first is considered an irrevocable offer within the meaning of article 1329 ...

La. Civ. C.

Art. 2620: An option to buy, or an option to sell, is a contract whereby a party gives to another the right to accept an offer to sell, or to by, a thing within a stipulated time ...

Art. 2625: A party may agree that he will not sell a certain thing without first offering it to a certain person. The right given to the latter in such a case is a right of first refusal that may be enforced by specific performance.

2. At Common Law

G.H. Treitel
(opus cited)

A unilateral contract may arise when one party promises to pay the other a sum of money if the other will do (or forbear from doing) something without making any promise to that effect: for example, when one person promises to pay another L100 if he will walk from London to York, or find and return the promisor's dog, or give up smoking for a year. In these cases the contract is described as unilateral as the promisee has clearly made no counter-promise to performed the required act or forbearance; ...

Once a promise is classified as an offer of a unilateral contract, a number of rules apply to the acceptance of such an offer.... [13]

Butterworths Common Law Series, The Law of Contract, 2007
Offer and Acceptance in Unilateral Contracts

Nature of Unilateral Contract

2.253   A unilateral contract arises where one party makes a promise to another undertaking to do, or to refrain from doing, something if the party to whom the promise is made does or refrains from doing something in return. Such contracts are therefore sometimes referred to as "if" contracts. They are unilateral because only one party makes a promise and therefore only one comes under a legal obligation. If the promisee performs or forbears in accordance with the promisor's stipulation, the promisor is bound; but the

---

13. G.H. Treitel p.30–34.

promisee never undertakes to do or refrain from doing anything and is therefore never under any legal obligation.[14]

E. Allan Farnsworth

(opus cited)

§ 3.4. **Bilateral and Unilateral Contracts.** Traditional analysis of the bargaining process developed a dichotomy between "bilateral" and "unilateral" contracts. In forming a bilateral contract each party makes a promise: the offeror makes the promise contained in the offer, and the offeree makes a promise in return as acceptance.... In forming a unilateral contract only one party makes a promise: the offeror makes the promise contained in the offer, and the offeree renders some performance as acceptance.... Traditional analysis has it that in a bilateral contract there are promises on both sides..; there are *duties* on both sides ... and *rights* on both sides ... In a unilateral contract, however, there is a promise on only one side ... ; there is a *duty* on only one side ... and a *right* on the other side ...

The dichotomy between bilateral and unilateral plays a less important role in contemporary analysis of contracts. The Restatement Second abandons the use of the terms because of "doubts as to the utility of the distinction," which causes "confusion in cases where performance is complete on one side except for an incidental or collateral promise, as where an offer to buy goods is accepted by shipment and a warranty is implied.[15]

Restatement, 2d

§ 45. Option Contract Created by Part Performance or Tender

(1) Where an offer invites an offeree to accept by rendering a performance and does not invite a promissory acceptance, an option contract is created when the offeree tenders or begins the invited performance or tenders a beginning of it.

(2) The offeror's duty of performance under any option contract so created is conditional on completion or tender of the invited performance in accordance with the terms of the offer.

---

14. p.512.
15. E. Allan Farnsworth, supra, at p.111–112.

Comment: a…. Such an offer has often been referred to as an "offer for a unilateral contract." Typical illustrations are found in offers of rewards or prizes and in non-commercial arrangements among relatives and friends.

B: Onerous Contracts and Gratuitous Contracts

1. At Civil Law

a: Concepts

Fr. Civ. C.

Art. 1105: A contract is gratuitous when one party intends to provide an advantage to the other without receiving an advantage in return.

Art. 1106: A contract is onerous when each of the parties expects to receive from the other an advantage in exchange for the advantage she herself provides.

La. Civ. C.

Art. 1909: A contract is onerous when each of the parties obtains an advantage in exchange for his obligation.

Art. 1910: A contract is gratuitous when one party obligates himself towards another for the benefit of the latter, without obtaining any advantage in return.

C.C.Q.

Art. 1381: A contract is onerous when each party obtains an advantage in return for his obligation.

When one party obligates himself to the other for the benefit of the latter without obtaining any advantage in return, the contract is gratuitous.

b: Illustrations

It. Civ. C.

Art. 769: A gift is a contract by which, in the spirit of liberality, one party enriches the other, disposing of one of his rights in the other's favor or assuming an obligation toward him.

BGB

Section 516: (1) A bestowal by means of which someone enriches another person from his own assets, is a donation if both parties are in agreement that the bestowal occurs without remuneration....

Sw. Fed. C.O.

see **Article 239**, supra p.29.

Art. 184: A contract of sale is a contract whereby the seller agrees to deliver the property sold to the buyer and to transfer the ownership therein to him and whereby the buyer agrees to pay to the seller the purchase price ...

La. Civ. C.

Art. 2343.1: The transfer by a spouse to the other spouse of a thing forming part of his separate property, with the stipulation that it shall be part of the community, transforms the thing into community property. As to both movables and immovables, a transfer by onerous title must be made in writing and a transfer by gratuitous title must be made by authentic act.

2. At Common Law

Wm. Blackstone, Commentaries on the Laws of England
by G.Chase, LL.B. 1890 (at p.546, 547, 553)

[...] *gifts* are always *gratuitous, grants* are upon some *consideration* or equivalent; ... A true and proper gift or grant is always accompanied with delivery of possession, and takes effect immediately: as if A. gives to B. 100L, or a flock of sheep, and puts him in possession of them directly, it is then a gift executed in the donee; ... But if the gift does not take effect, by delivery of immediate possession, it is then not properly a gift, but a contract; and this a man cannot be compelled to perform, but upon good an sufficient consideration ...

I. Sale, or *exchange*, is a transmutation of property from one man to another, in consideration of some price or recompense in value: for there is no sale without a recompense: there must be *quid pro quo*.

P.S. Atiyah, An Introduction to The Law of Contract

4th ed. Clarendon Press, 1989 (at p.157–160)

7. THE FUTURE OF THE DOCTRINE OF CONSIDERATION[16]

[...] At the end of the day,...,we must recognize the point made much earlier, that the doctrine of consideration often operates as a paternalistic device, limiting the freedom of parties in private relationships. The limits are not very serious because in most cases a person who quite calculatedly and deliberately seeks to incur a gratuitous obligation can easily give effect to his legal intentions. There is, of course, nothing in the doctrine which prevents a person from making a gift; all that the doctrine does is to make it difficult— though not impossible—to bind oneself by a *promise* to make a gift ...

G.H. Treitel

(opus cited)

Consideration[17]: The basic feature of that doctrine is the idea of reciprocity: "something of value in the eye of the law" must be given for a promise in order to make it enforceable as a contract. An informal gratuitous promise therefore does not amount to a contract. A person or body to whom a promise of a gift is made from purely charitable or sentimental motives gives nothing for the promise; and the claims of such a promisee are obviously less compelling than those of a person who has given (or promised) some return for the promise.... Such promises ... may be rashly made; and the requirements of executing a deed or giving value provide at least some protection against this danger.

Restatement, 2d

§ 86. Promise for Benefit Received

(1) A promise made in recognition of a benefit previously received by the promisor from the promisee is binding to the extent necessary to prevent injustice.

(2) A promise is not binding under Subsection (1)

(a) if the promisee conferred the benefit as a gift or for other reasons the promisor has not been unjustly enriched; or

---

16. On cause and consideration , see below p.79–98.
17. p.52–53.

(b) to the extent that its value is disproportionate to the benefit.

§ 90. Promise Reasonably Inducing Action or Forbearance

(1) A promise which the promisor should reasonably expect to induce action or forbearance on the part of the promisee or a third person and which does induce such action or forbearance is binding if injustice can be avoided only by enforcement of the promise. The remedy granted for breach may be limited as justice requires ...

E. Allan Farnsworth
(opus cited)

§ 2.5 Exchange Lacking: Gratuitous Promises.

The most significant class of promises unenforceable for lack of consideration is made up of purely gratuitous (or gift) promises — promises for which there has been no exchange at all.... Our common law tradition, in contrast to that of civil law systems, does not require us to define a special category of promises regarded as gratuitous. As far as enforceability is concerned, what is significant is not that a promise is gratuitous but that it lacks consideration.

A gift (a present transfer of an interest in property) stands on a footing different from that of a promise to make a gift.[...] once the gift has been completed by the donor's delivery (of the watch), the transfer is irrevocable and the donor cannot recover it ... Why should delivery make a difference? To say that the promise to make a gift is governed by the law of contracts while the gift is governed by the law of property is scarcely satisfactory ... Whatever its justification, the distinction remains. It accounts for the most important type of promise that lacks consideration, the purely gratuitous promise — the promise for which there has been no exchange at all ...

Part I
Formation of Contracts

Chapter Four

Offer and Acceptance

In both the civil law and the common law systems, an agreement between two parties becomes a contract when it is intended to create legally binding obligations on the parties. In addition to other requirements which may not all be identical between the two major legal systems, the intention or will of the parties must clearly be to enter into a bond of law which is meant to give rise to obligations as distinguished from a mere "invitation to treat."[18]

"There is ... no doubt that it is essential to the creation of a contract, using this word in its legal sense, that the parties to an agreement shall not only be ad item as to the terms of their agreement, but that they shall have intended that it shall have legal consequences and be legally enforceable."[19] "[I]t is quite possible for parties to come to an agreement by accepting a proposal with the result that the agreement concluded does not give rise to legal relations. The reason is that the parties do not intend that their agreement shall give rise to legal relations. This intention may be implied from the subject matter of the agreement, but it may also be expressed by the parties. In social and family relations such an intention is readily implied, while in business matters the opposite result would ordinarily follow."[20] "To create a contract there must be a common intention of the parties to enter into legal obligations, mutually communicated expressly or impliedly. Such an intention ordinarily will be inferred when parties enter into an agreement which in other respects conforms to the rules of law as to the formation of contracts."[21]

This "common intention" necessary for the parties to enter into legal obligations is made up of "consent" (terminology mostly used in civil law systems) consisting in an "offer and its acceptance" (terminology mostly used in

---

18. G.H.Treitel p.8.
19. Bankes L.J. in Rose and Frank Co. v. J.R. Crompton and Brothers Ltd [1923] 2 K.B. 261 at 282.
20. Scrutton L.J. id. At 288.
21. Atkin L.J. id. At 293.

common law) and the reaching of a "common intention." One also speaks of the "meeting of the minds" of the parties who have shared with each other that "common intention" by some means of communication.

Both in the civil law and the common law, for the expression of man's will to amount to an "offer" so as to lead, upon its acceptance, to the creation of a bond of law, that "offer" must meet some fundamental requirements. Likewise, for an "acceptance" of an "offer" to "meet" that "offer" and lead to a binding agreement, the "acceptance" itself must meet the same fundamental requirements. At that point in time when the acceptance meets the offer the parties reach a *consensus at idem*, or agreement to the same thing, which binds the parties, assuming that the other requirements for a contract are met, such as the integrity of the parties' wills, or the cause or consideration which distinctive requirements will be discussed below.

§ 1 When Is an Offer, an "Offer" in a Legal Sense?

A: Civil Law

La. Civ. C.

Art. 1927: A contract is formed by the consent of the parties established through offer and acceptance.

Unless the law prescribes a certain formality for the intended contract, offer and acceptance may be made orally, in writing, or by action or inaction that under the circumstances is clearly indicative of consent.

Art. 1928: An offer that specifies a period of time for acceptance is irrevocable during that time.

Fr. Civ. C.

Art. 1108: Four requirements are essential for the validity of a convention:

-the consent of the party who binds herself.

BGB

§116: A declaration of intent is not void by virtue of the fact that the declarant has made a mental reservation of not wanting the declaration made. The declaration is void if it is to be made to another who knows of the reservation.

§118: A declaration of intent not seriously intended which is made in the expectation that it will be understood not to be seriously intended is void.

§145: Any person who offers to another to enter into a contract is bound by the offer, unless he has excluded being bound to it.

Sw. Fed. C.O.

Art. 3: Where a person offers to another to enter into a contract and fixes a time for acceptance of such offer, such person is bound by his offer until the expiration of the said time limit.

He is only released if he does not, before the expiration of such time limit, receive from the other party notice of acceptance.

Art. 7: The offeror is not bound where he adds to the offer a declaration declining liability, or where such reservation results from the nature of the transaction or the circumstances.

The despatch of tariffs, price lists or similar items does not constitute an offer.

But the display of goods with price-quotation is considered as a rule as an offer.

Art. 8(1): A person who offers publicly a reward for an act is bound to discharge this reward in accordance with the terms thereof.

C.C.Q.

Art. 1388: An offer to contract is a proposal which contains all the essential of the proposed contract and in which the offeror signifies his willingness to be bound if it is accepted.

Art. 1389: An offer to contract derives from the person who initiates the contract or the person who determines its content or even, in certain cases, the person who presents the last essential element of the proposed contract.

B: Common law

Restatement, 2d

§ 24. Offer Defined

An offer is the manifestation of willingness to enter into a bargain, so made as to justify another person in understanding that his assent to that bargain is invited and will conclude it.

§ 26. Preliminary Negotiations

A manifestation of willingness to enter into a bargain is not an offer if the person to whom it is addressed knows or has reason to know that the person making it does not intend to conclude a bargain until he has made a further manifestation of assent.

§ 33. Certainty

(1) Even though a manifestation of intention is intended to be understood as an offer, it cannot be accepted so as to form a contract unless the terms of the contract are reasonably certain.

(2) The terms of a contract are reasonably certain if they provide a basis for determining the existence of a breach and for giving an appropriate remedy.

(3) The fact that one or more terms of a proposed bargain are left open or uncertain may show that a manifestation of intention is not intended to be understood as an offer or as an acceptance.

§ 35. The Offeree's Power of Acceptance

(1) An offer gives to the offeree a continuing power to complete the manifestation of mutual assent by acceptance of the offer.

(2) A contract cannot be created by acceptance of an offer after the power of acceptance has been terminated in one of the ways listed in §36.

§ 39. Counter-offers

(1) A counter-offer is an offer made by an offeree to his offeror relating to the same matter as the original offer and proposing a substituted bargain differing from that proposed by the original offer.

UCC

§ 205: An offer by a merchant to buy or sell goods in a signed record that by its terms gives assurance that it will be held open is not revocable, for lack of consideration, during the time stated or if no time is stated for a reasonable time, but in no event may the period of irrevocability exceed three months. Any such term of assurance in a form supplied by the offeree must be separately signed by the offeror.

E. Allan Farnsworth
(opus cited)

§3.3. Offer and Acceptance.

What is an "offer"? It can be defined as a manifestation to another of assent to enter into a contract if the other manifests assent in return by some action, often a promise but sometimes a performance. By making an offer, the offeror thus confers upon the offeree the power to create a contract.... *Offer,* then, is the name given to a promise that is conditioned on some action by the promisee *if* the legal effect of the promisee's taking that action is to make the promisee enforceable. Empowerment of the offeree to make the offeror's promise enforceable is thus the essence of an offer ...

G.H. Treitel
(opus cited)

CHAPTER 2, AGREEMENT, *SECTION 1. OFFER [at p.7 et seq.]*

1. Offer Defined

An offer is an expression of willingness to contract on certain terms made with the intention that it shall become binding as soon as it is accepted by the person to whom it is addressed ...

2. Offer Distinguished from Invitation to Treat

The question whether a statement is an offer or an invitation to treat depends primarily on the intention with which it is made.... [A] statement is not an offer if it in terms negatives the maker's intention to be bound on acceptance; ... a statement may be an invitation to treat, although it contains the word "offer"; while a statement may be an offer although it is expressed to be an "acceptance," or although it requests the person to whom it is addressed to make an "offer."

The distinction between an offer and an invitation to treat is often hard to draw as it depends on the elusive criterion of intention.

Butterworths

(opus cited)

Offer

Introduction

2.195   An offer consists of an indication, by words or by conduct, that the person making it—the offeror—is willing to accept a legal obligation to do, or to refrain from doing, something if the person to whom it is addresses— the offeree—agrees to its terms. If the offeree accepts the offer by agreeing to its terms and providing the consideration requested by the offeror, it will give rise to a contract which will impose legally binding obligations on the offeror and, depending on the nature of the offer, the offeree. If the offer is of a bilateral contract, it will when accepted bind both parties; if of a unilateral contract (or 'if' contract, as it is sometimes described), it will bind only the offeror.

C: International/Multinational

UNIDROIT

Art. 2.1.2: *(Definition of offer):* A proposal for concluding a contract constitutes an offer if it is sufficiently definite and indicates the intention of the offeror to be bound in case of acceptance.

Art. 2.1.13: *(Conclusion of contract dependent on agreement on specific matters or in a particular form):* Where in the course of negotiations one of the parties insists that the contract is not concluded until there is agreement on specific matters or in a particular form, no contract is concluded before agreement is reached on those matters or in that form.

CISG

14(1): A proposal for concluding a contract addressed to one or more specific persons constitutes an offer if it is sufficiently definite and indicates the

intention of the offeror to be bound in case of acceptance. A proposal is sufficiently definite if it indicates the goods and expressly or implicitly fixes or
makes provision for determining the quantity and the price.

(2) A proposal other than one addressed to one or more specific persons is
to be considered merely as an invitation to make offers, unless the contrary is
clearly indicated by the person making the proposal.

Principles of European Contract Law

ARTICLE 2-201: OFFER

(1) A proposal amounts to an offer if:

(a) it is intended to result in a contract if the other party accepts it, and

(b) it contains sufficiently definite terms to form a contract.

(2) An offer may be made to one or more specific persons or to the public.

ARTICLE 2-103: SUFFICIENT AGREEMENT

(1)There is sufficient agreement if the terms:

(a) have been sufficiently defined by the parties so that the contract can
be enforced, or

(b) can be determined under these Principles

(2) However, if one of the parties refuses to conclude a contract unless the
parties have agreed on some specific matter, there is no contract unless
agreement on that matter has been reached.

§2 When Is an Acceptance, an "Acceptance" in a Legal Sense?

A: Civil Law

La. Civ. C.

Art. 1927: Unless the law prescribes a certain formality for the intended
contract, offer and acceptance may be made orally, in writing, or by action
or inaction that under the circumstances is clearly indicative of consent.

Unless otherwise specified in the offer, there need not be conformity between the manner in which the offer is made and the manner in which the acceptance is made.

Art. 1928: An offer that specifies a period of time for acceptance is irrevocable during that time.

Art. 1939: When an offeror invites an offeree to accept by performance and, according to usage or the nature or the terms of the contract, it is contemplated that the performance will be completed if commenced, a contract is formed when the offeree begins the requested performance.

Art. 1942: When, because of special circumstances, the offeree's silence leads the offeror reasonably to believe that a contract has been formed, the offer is deemed accepted.

Art. 1943: An acceptance not in accordance with the terms of the offer is deemed to be a counteroffer.[22]

BGB

§ 150: (1) The late acceptance of an offer is deemed to be a new offer.

(2) An acceptance with expansions, restrictions or other alterations is deemed to be a rejection combined with a new offer."

§ 154: (1) Until the parties have agreed on all points of a contract on which an agreement was required to be reached according to the declaration of even only one party, the contract is, in case of doubt, not entered into. An agreement on individual points is not legally binding, even if they have been recorded.

§ 155: If the parties to a contract which they regard to have concluded have, in fact, not agreed on a point on which an agreement was required to be reached, whatever is agreed is applicable if it may be assumed that the

---

22. Example: **La.Civ.C. Art. 2721:** A lease with a fixed term is reconducted if, after the expiration of the term, and without notice to vacate or terminate or other opposition by the lessor or the lessee, the lessee remains in possession:
(1) For thirty days in the case of an agricultural lease;
(2) For one week in the case of other leases with a fixed term that is no longer than a week; or
(3) For one day in the case of a lease with a fixed term that is equal to or shorter than a week.

contract would have been concluded even without a provision concerning this point.

C.C.Q.

Art. 1393: An acceptance which does not correspond substantially to the offer or which is received by the offeror after the offer has lapsed does not constitute acceptance.

It may, however, constitute a new offer.

B: Common Law

G.H. Treitel
(opus cited)

1. Acceptance Defined

An acceptance is a final and unqualified expression of assent to the terms of an offer. The objective test of agreement applies to an acceptance no less than to an offer. On this test, a mere acknowledgment of an offer would not be an acceptance; nor is there an acceptance where a person who has received an offer to sell goods merely replies that it is his "intention to place an order..... .

(3) Acceptance by conduct

An offer may be accepted by conduct, e.g. by dispatching goods in response to an offer to buy ... Conduct will, however, only have this effect if the offeree did the act with the intention of accepting the offer ...

(4) Acceptance must be unqualified

A communication may fail to take effect as an acceptance because it attempts to vary the terms of the offer.

The requirement that the acceptance must be unqualified does not, however, mean that there must be verbal correspondence between offer and acceptance.... [A] reply which adds some new provision by way of indulgence to the offeror may be an acceptance.... [A]n acceptance may be effective although the acceptor asks for extra time to pay, so long as he makes it clear that he is prepared to perform in accordance with the terms of the offer even if his request is refused ...

Butterworths

(opus cited)

2.195 [...]An acceptance is a response to an offer which unequivocally and without qualification, addition or reservation agrees to all of the terms of the offer. It follows therefore that in order to be an offer a proposal must be capable of maturing into a binding contract without further negotiation, and so must at least indicate the minimum terms necessary to give rise to a binding and enforceable contract[...]

2.224 Express acceptance Acceptance will be inferred if the offeree responds to the offer with any words which, viewed objectively, indicate his unequivocal assent to all the terms of the offer. It is not necessary for the offeree to use any particular formula such as "I accept".

2.225 Acceptance by conduct Acceptance may also be inferred from conduct so that the offeree will be deemed to have accepted if he does any act ... which, viewed objectively and in context, unequivocally indicates his intention to agree to ... and be bound by, the terms of the offer.[...]

2.226 Conduct must be unequivocal Acceptance will only be inferred if the conduct of the offeree points unequivocally to an intention to accept the offer; the court will not impose a contract on the parties.[...]

2.227 Acceptance by silence [...] The question whether silence can constitute acceptance is unlikely to arise in the abstract. It will normally arise where one party alleges that there is a contract on particular terms and the other denies it on the grounds that there was no effective acceptance. [...] [T]here could be circumstances in which silence could constitute acceptance binding on the offeree....

2.228 Can the offeree be bound by his silence? The offeree should be bound by his silence where he has undertaken a duty to speak. There is then no question of imposition of a contract.[...]

2.229 Can the offeror be bound by the offeree's silence? There may be good reasons for saying that generally the offeree should not be bound by silent inactivity.[...]

2.230 The difficulty in treating silence as acceptance is that silence is rarely unequivocal. However, it will be rare that an attempt is made to infer a contract from silence and inactivity. In many cases one party's silent inactivity following an offer may be equated to conduct from which acceptance may reasonably be inferred.[...]

Restatement, 2d

§ 30. Form of Acceptance Invited

(1) An offer may invite or require acceptance to be made by an affirmative answer in words, or by performing or refraining from performing a specified act, or may empower the offeree to make a selection of terms in his acceptance.

(2) Unless otherwise indicated by the language or the circumstances, an offer invites acceptance in any manner and by any medium reasonable in the circumstances.

§ 32. Invitation of Promise or Performance

In case of doubt an offer is interpreted as inviting the offeree to accept either by promising to perform what the offer requests or by rendering the performance, as the offeree chooses.

§ 35. The Offeree's Power of Acceptance

See supra p.42.

§ 39. Counter-offers

(2) An offeree's power of acceptance is terminated by his making of a counter-offer, unless the offeror has manifested a contrary intention or unless the counter-offer manifests a contrary intention of the offeree.

§ 58. Necessity of Acceptance Complying with Terms of Offer

An acceptance must comply with the requirements of the offer as to the promise to be made or the performance to be rendered.

§ 59. Purported Acceptance Which Adds Qualifications

A reply to an offer which purports to accept it but is conditional on the offeror's assent to terms additional to or different from those offered is not an acceptance but is a counter-offer.

UCC

§ 2-206. Offer and Acceptance in Formation of Contract.

(1) Unless otherwise unambiguously indicated by the language or circumstances

(a) an offer to make a contract shall be construed as inviting acceptance in any manner and by any medium reasonable in the circumstances:

(b) an order or other offer to buy goods for prompt or current shipment shall be construed as inviting acceptance either by a prompt promise to ship or by the prompt or current shipment of conforming or nonconforming goods, but the shipment of nonconforming goods is not an acceptance if the seller seasonably notifies the buyer that the shipment is offered only as an accommodation to the buyer.

(2) If the beginning of a requested performance is a reasonable mode of acceptance, an offeror that is not notified of acceptance within a reasonable time may treat the offer as having lapsed before acceptance.

(3) A definite and seasonable expression of acceptance in a record operates as an acceptance even if it contains terms additional to or different from the offer.

§ 2-207. Terms of Contract; Effect of Confirmation.

Subject to Section 2-202, if (i) conduct by both parties recognizes the existence of a contract although their records do not otherwise establish a contract, (ii) a contract is formed by an offer and acceptance, or (iii) a contract formed in any manner is confirmed by a record that contains terms additional to or different from those in the contract being confirmed, the terms of the contract are:

(a) terms that appear in the records of both parties;

(b) terms, whether in a record or not, to which both parties agree; and

(c) terms supplied or incorporated under any provision of this Act.

E. Allan Farnsworth

(opus cited)

§3.3 Offer and Acceptance ... What is an acceptance? It can be defined as the action (promise or performance) by the offeree that creates a contract (i.e. makes the offeror's promise enforceable). *Acceptance*, then, is the name given to the offeree's action if the legal effect of that action is to make the offeror's promise enforceable.

C. International/Multinational

UNIDROIT

Art. 2.1.6 (Mode of acceptance)

(1) A statement made by or other conduct of the offeree indicating assent to an offer is an acceptance.

(3) However, if, by virtue of the offer or as a result of practices which the parties have established between themselves or of usage, the offeree may indicate assent by performing an act without notice to the offeror, the acceptance is effective when the act is performed.

Art. 2.1.11 (Modified acceptance)

(1) A reply to an offer which purports to be an acceptance but contains additions, limitations or other modifications is a rejection of the offer and constitutes a counter-offer.

(2) However, a reply to an offer which purports to be an acceptance but contains additional or different terms which do not materially alter the terms of the offer constitutes an acceptance, unless the offeror, without undue delay, objects to the discrepancy. If the offeror does not object, the terms of the contract are the terms of the offer with the modifications contained in the acceptance.

CISG

Article 19

(1) A reply to an offer which purports to be an acceptance but contains additions, limitations or other modifications is a rejection of the offer and constitutes a counteroffer.

(2) However, a reply to an offer which purports to be an acceptance but contains additional or different terms which do not materially alter the terms of the offer constitutes an acceptance, unless the offeror, without undue delay, objects orally to the discrepancy or dispatches a notice to that effect. If he does not so object, the terms of the contract are the terms of the offer with the modifications contained in the acceptance.

(3) Additional or different terms relating, among other things, to the price, payment, quality and quantity of the goods, place and time of deliv-

ery, extent of one party's liability to the other or the settlement of disputes are considered to alter the terms of the offer materially."

Principles of European Contract Law

Article 2:208: MODIFIED ACCEPTANCE

(1) "A reply by the offeree which states or implies additional or different terms which would materially alter the terms of the offer is a rejection and a new offer.

(2) A reply which gives a definite assent to an offer operates as an acceptance even if it states or implies additional or different terms, provided these do not materially alter the terms of the offer. The additional or different terms then become part of the contract.

(3) However, such a reply will be treated as a rejection of the offer if:

(a) the offer expressly limits acceptance to the terms of the offer; or

(b) the offeror objects to the additional or different terms without delay; or

(c) the offeree makes its acceptance conditional upon the offeror's assent to the additional or different terms, and the assent does not reach the offeree within a reasonable time."

§ 3. Meeting of the Minds; *Consensus ad idem*

As a general rule, an acceptance must be communicated to the offeror for a meeting of the minds to occur and to make up this essential element of the creation of a bond of law. The issue to be addressed now is that of the nature of the 'communication' of the acceptance that is to say the form or forms such a communication of the acceptance can take so as to bind the parties. Because of practical, business, commercial ... reasons, both the civil law and the common law have had to consider different forms of communication and determine their respective impact on achieving one single and fundamental objective: the meeting of the minds of the parties, their consensus ad idem.

A: Forms of Acceptance

1. Civil Law

La. Civ. C.

Art. 1927: (2): see supra p.40.

Art. 1936: A medium or a manner of acceptance is reasonable if it is the one used in making the offer or one customary in similar transactions at the time and place the offer is received, unless circumstances known to the offeree indicate otherwise.

Art. 1939: see supra p.46.

Art. 1940: When, according to usage or the nature of the contract, or its own terms, an offer made to a particular offeree can be accepted only by rendering a completed performance, the offeror cannot revoke the offer, once the offeree has begun to perform, for the reasonable time necessary to complete the performance. The offeree, however, is not bound to complete the performance he has begun.

The offeror's duty of performance is conditional on completion or tender of the requested performance.

Art. 1941: When commencement of the performance either constitutes acceptance or makes the offer irrevocable, the offeree must give prompt notice of that commencement unless the offeror knows or should know that the offeree has begun to perform. An offeree who fails to give the notice is liable for damages.

Art. 1942: see supra p.46.

Fr. Civ. C.

Art. 2015: Suretyship is not presumed; it must be expressly stated, and it cannot be extended beyond the limits within which it was contracted.

C.C.Q.

Art. 1387: A contract is formed when and where acceptance is received by the offeror, regardless of the method of communication used, and even though the parties have agreed to reserve agreement as to secondary terms.

Art. 1394: Silence does not imply acceptance of an offer, subject only to the will of the parties, the law or special circumstances, such as usage or a prior business relationship.

BGB

§ 151: A contract comes into existence through the acceptance of the offer without the offeror needing to be notified of acceptance, if such a declaration is not to be expected according to common usage, or if the offeror has waved it. The moment when the offer expires is determined according to the intention of the offeror which is to be inferred from the offer or the circumstances.

2. Common Law

G.H. Treitel
(opus cited, p.18 et seq)

2. Communication of Acceptance

(1) General rule

The general rule is that an acceptance has no effect until it is communicated to the offeror. One reason for this rule is the difficulty of proving an uncommunicated decision to accept "for the Devil himself knows not the intent of a man" ... The main reason for the rule is that it could cause hardship to an offeror if he were bound without knowing that his offer had been accepted ...

An acceptance is "communicated" when it is actually brought to the notice of the offeror ...

(2) Exceptional Cases

"In a number of cases, an acceptance is, or may be, effective although it is not brought to the notice of the offeror.

(a) COMMUNICATION TO OFFEROR'S AGENT ...

(b) CONDUCT OF OFFEROR ...

(d) ACCEPTANCE BY POST ..."

(2) Alternative method: silence.

(a) OFFEREE GENERALLY NOT BOUND. In general, an offeree who simply does nothing on receipt of an offer which states that it may be accepted by silence is not bound.... [T]here may be exceptions to the general rule that an offeree is not bound by silence.... Even where silence of the offeree does not amount to an acceptance, it is arguable that he might be liable on a different basis (... on a kind of estoppel) ... But such an estoppel can only arise out of clear and unequivocal representation ... ;..mere inactivity is not generally sufficient, so that silence in response to an offer will not normally give rise to an estoppel.

(b) OFFEROR BOUND? There is some authority for saying that the offeror cannot, any more than the offeree, be bound where the offeree simply remains silent in response to the offer.

Butterworths

(opus cited)

COMMUNICATION OF ACCEPTANCE

2.240 The general rule is that if it is to be effective, acceptance must be communicated to the offeror. [...] as Lord Denning observed, if the rule were otherwise, offerees would be able to 'play fast and loose as they pleased.'[...]

2.241 Mode of communication of acceptance In general, notice of acceptance can be given to the offeror by any means. However, it is open to the offeror to stipulate in the offer for acceptance to be communicated in a particular way.[...]

WHEN IS COMMUNICATION EFFECTIVE?

2.243 [...] The general rule is that acceptance is not effective until communicated to the offeror. That rule is, however, subject to an important qualification when acceptance is notified through the medium of the post.

2.244 Acceptance sent by post It was decided in Adams v. Lindsell that a posted letter of acceptance takes effect at the time of posting and by 1880 the rule was treated as settled law.... The letter of acceptance is effective once it is in the control of the Post Office.

It is generally recognized that the rule that a posted acceptance is effective on posting is anomalous. Various attempts have [been] made to justify it. In Adams v. Lindsell itself it was explained on the basis of the need for finality, and that if the rule were that a posted acceptance must reach the offeror:.

> ... *no contract could ever be completed by the post. For if the defendants were not bound by their offer when accepted by the plaintiffs till the answer*

was received, then the plaintiffs ought not to be bound till after they had re-ceived the notification that the defendants had received their answer and assented to it. And so it might go on ad infinitum.

2.249 Other forms of communication The postal acceptance rule has been applied to telegrams of acceptance.[...] The postal rule only applies where the post is the proper, or anticipated, method of communication.[...] It should be remembered that the postal rule is an exception to the general rule that communication of the acceptance must be made to the offeror, ... The courts have refused to extend the anomalous postal rule to other forms of communication at a distance such as telex or fax.

Restatement, 2d

§ 50. Acceptance of Offer defined; Acceptance by Performance; Acceptance by Promise

(1) Acceptance of an offer is a manifestation of assent to the terms thereof made by the offeree in a manner invited or required by the offer.

(2) Acceptance by performance requires that at least part of what the offer requests be performed or tendered and includes acceptance by a performance which operates as a return promise.

(3) Acceptance by a promise requires that the offeree complete every act essential to the making of the promise.

§ 54. Acceptance by Performance; Necessity of Notification to Offeror

(1)Where an offer invites an offeree to accept by rendering a performance, no notification is necessary to make such an acceptance effective unless the offer requests such a notification.

(2) If an offeree who accepts by rendering a performance has reason to know that the offeror has no adequate means of learning of the performance with reasonable promptness and certainty, the contractual duty of the offeror is discharged unless

(a) the offeree exercises reasonable diligence to notify the offeror of ac-ceptance, or

(b) the offeror learns of the performance within a reasonable time, or

(c) the offer indicates that notification of acceptance is not required.

§65. Reasonableness of Medium of Acceptance

Unless circumstances known to the offeree indicate otherwise, a medium of acceptance is reasonable if it is the one used by the offeror or one customary in similar transactions at the time and place the offer is received.

§69. Acceptance by Silence or Exercise of Dominion

(1) Where an offeree fails to reply to an offer, his silence and inaction operate as an acceptance in the following cases only:

(a) Where an offeree takes the benefit of offered services with reasonable opportunity to reject them and reason to know that they were offered with the expectation of compensation ...

(b) Where the offeror has stated or given the offeree reason to understand that assent may be manifested by silence or inaction, and the offeree in remaining silent and inactive intends to accept the offer.

(c) Where because of previous dealings or otherwise, it is reasonable that the offeree should notify the offeror if he does not intend to accept.

(2) An offeree who does any act inconsistent with the offeror's ownership of offered property is bound in accordance with the offered terms unless they are manifestly unreasonable. But if the act is wrongful as against the offeror it is an acceptance only if ratified by him.

UCC

§1-201 (3) "Agreement," as distinguished from "contract," means the bargain of the parties in fact, as found in their language or inferred from other circumstances, including course of performance, course of dealing, or usage of trade as provided in Section 1-303.

§1-303. Course of Performance, Course of Dealing, and Usage of Trade.

(a) A "course of performance" is a sequence of conduct between the parties to a particular transaction that exists if:

(1) the agreement of the parties with respect to the transaction involves repeated occasions for performance by a party; and

(2) the other party, with knowledge of the nature of the performance and opportunity for objection to it, accepts the performance or acquiesces in it without objection.

(b) A "course of dealing" is a sequence of conduct concerning previous transactions between the parties to a particular transaction that is fairly to be regarded as establishing a common basis of understanding for interpreting their expressions and other conduct.

(c) A "usage of trade" is any practice or method of dealing ... as to justify an expectation that it will be observed with respect to the transaction in question....

§ 2-207. Terms of Contract; Effect of Confirmation.

Subject to Section 2-202, if (i) conduct by both parties recognizes the existence of a contract although their records do not otherwise establish a contract, (ii) a contract is formed by an offer and acceptance, or (iii) a contract formed in any manner is confirmed by a record that contains terms additional to or different from those in the contract being confirmed, the terms of the contract are:

(a) terms that appear in the records of both parties;

(b) terms, whether in a record or not, to which both parties agree; and

(c) terms supplied or incorporated under any provision of this Act."

E. Allan Farnsworth
(opus cited)

§3.1. Requirements of Assent and of Definiteness. [...]

The first requirement, that of assent, follows from the premise that contractual liability is consensual. Since it is difficult for a workable system of contract law to take account of assent unless there has been an overt expression of it, courts have required that assent to the formation of a contract be manifested in some way, by words or other conduct, if it is to be effective ...

§3.14. Promise Inferred from Silence or Exercise of Dominion

As a general rule, a promise will not be inferred from the offeree's mere inaction. Thus an offeree's silence in the face of an offer to sell goods is not ordinarily an acceptance, because the offeror has no reason to believe from the offeree's silence that the offeree promises to buy. The same is true if the offeror delivers the goods to the offeree, which retains them in silence. If there are additional circumstances, however, a promise may be inferred, resulting in a contract that is sometimes described as "implied-in-fact" as distinguished from "express."[...]

So fundamental is the tenet that mere silence is not acceptance that, even as the master of the offer, the offeror is powerless to alter the rule.[...]

There are, however, exceptional situations in which silence has been held to be an acceptance. Although courts occasionally talk of a "duty to speak," a sounder rationale is that in these situations the offeror has reason to believe from the offeree's silence that the offeree assents. Each case turns on its own facts.[...]

3. International/Multinational

UNIDROIT

Article 2.1.6 (see supra p.51)

Principles of European Contract Law

Article 2:204: ACCEPTANCE

(1) Any form of statement or conduct by the offeree is an acceptance if it indicates assent to the offer

(2) Silence or inactivity does not in itself amount to acceptance.

CISG

Article 18

(1) A statement made by or other conduct of the offeree indicating assent to an offer is an acceptance. Silence or inactivity does not in itself amount to an acceptance.

(3) However, if, by virtue of the offer or as a result of practices which the parties have established between themselves or of usage, the offeree may indicate assent by performing an act, such as one relating to the dispatch of the goods or payment of the price, without notice to the offeror, the acceptance is effective at the moment the act is performed, provided that the act is performed within the period of time laid down in the preceding paragraph."

B: Meeting of the Minds: Revocable or Irrevocable Offer

Assuming that an "offer" on one side and an "acceptance" on the other side coincide, match each other in terms of content, and assuming that the acceptance has been "communicated," somehow, it remains to determine that exact moment in time when the acceptance "meets" the offer, when it can be said that the offeror has been made aware, actually or fictitiously, that the offeree has accepted the offer. The fundamental issue to address here is that of the revocable or the irrevocable offer. The civil law approach is, in general, to consider an offer as irrevocable, whereas the common law approach tends to favor the revocable offer. This dual approach to the issue of the timing of the formation of a contract is well illustrated in the elaborate principles adopted by international organizations. Four main theories or approaches are conceivable: the mailbox approach or dispatch theory; the transmission approach of an acceptance; the mere "expression or formulation" approach of the acceptance; the objective receipt theory or the receipt-information approach of an acceptance.

1. Civil Law

La. Civ. C.

Art. 1934: An acceptance of an irrevocable offer is effective when received by the offeror.

Art. 1935: Unless otherwise specified by the offer or the law, an acceptance of a revocable offer, made in a manner and by a medium suggested by the offer or in a reasonable manner and by a reasonable medium, is effective when transmitted by the offeree.

Art. 1937: A revocation of a revocable offer is effective when received by the offeree prior to acceptance.

BGB

§ 151. [see supra p.54]

Sw. Fed. C.O.

Art. 3 [see supra p.41].

Art. 4 Where the offer is made to a person present without a time limit being named, and such offer be not forthwith accepted, the offeror ceases to be bound.

Art. 6 Where, by reason of the special nature of the transaction, or having regard to the circumstances, an express acceptance is not to be expected, the contract is deemed to be binding unless the offer be refused within reasonable time.

Art. 10 "A contract entered into by absent parties takes effect at the time of the dispatch of the acceptance.

Where no express acceptance is necessary, the contract takes effect when the offer is received.

C.C.Q.

Art. 1392: An offer lapses if no acceptance is received by the offeror before the expiry of the specified term or, where no term is specified, before the expiry of a reasonable time; it also lapses in respect of the offeree if he has rejected it.

2. Common Law

G.H. Treitel

(opus cited p.18 et seq)

2. Communication of Acceptance

(2) Exceptional cases

(d) ACCEPTANCE BY POST. There are many possible solutions to the problem: when does a posted acceptance take effect? Such an acceptance could take effect when it is actually communicated to the offeror, when it arrives at his address, when it should, in the ordinary course of post, have reached him, or when it is posted.

(i) *The posting rule.* What is usually called the general rule is that a postal acceptance takes effect when the letter of acceptance is posted. For this purpose a letter is posted when it is in the control of the Post Office, or of one of its employees authorized to receive letters: handing a letter to a postman authorized to *deliver* letters is not posting.

(ii) *Reasons for the rule.* Various reasons for the rule have been suggested. One is that the offeror must be considered as making the offer all the time that his offer is in the post, and that therefore the agreement between the parties is complete as soon as the acceptance is posted.

Another suggested reason for the rule is that, if it did not exist "no contract could ever be completed by the post.... [23]

[...] But it would be perfectly possible to hold that the acceptance took effect when it came to the notice of the offeror, whether the offeree knew of this or not. Such a rule would not result in an infinity of letters. Yet another suggested reason for the rule is that the Post Office is the common agent of both parties, and that communication to this agent immediately completes the contract ...

The rule is in truth an arbitrary one, little better or worse than its competitors ... The rule does, however, serve a possibly useful function in limiting the offeror's power to withdraw his offer at will: It makes a posted acceptance binding although that acceptance only reaches the offeror after a previously posted withdrawal reaches the offeree."

Butterworths
(opus cited at p.510)

2.251 No absolute rule [...] the precise moment at which acceptance takes effect will take account of the conduct and the reasonable expectations of the parties ... The general rule means that communication by 'instantaneous' methods will not be regarded as effective *before* the time when it reaches the offeror's receiver. But where a message is sent by telex or fax or is left on a telephone answering machine, it may not actually come to the attention of the offeror for some time ... In the *Brinkibon* case Lord Wilberforce observed that: *No universal rule can cover all such cases; they must be resolved by reference to the intentions of the parties, by sound business practice and in some cases by a judgment where the risks should lie.*

---

23. see supra: Meeting of the Minds p.52.

[...] the acceptance should be effective when the offeree might reasonably expect it to come to the offeror's attention ...

Restatement, 2d

§ 63. Time When Acceptance Takes Effect

Unless the offer provides otherwise,

(a) an acceptance made in a manner and by a medium invited by an offer is operative and completes the manifestation of mutual assent as soon as put out of the offeree's possession, without regard to whether it ever reaches the offeror; but

(b) an acceptance under an option contract is not operative until received by the offeror.

§ 64. Acceptance by Telephone or Teletype

Acceptance given by telephone or other medium of substantially instantaneous two-way communication is governed by the principles applicable to acceptances where the parties are in the presence of each other.

§ 66. Acceptance Must be Properly Dispatched

An acceptance sent by mail or otherwise from a distance is not operative when dispatched, unless it is properly addressed and such other precautions taken as are ordinarily observed to insure safe transmission of similar messages.

§ 67. Effect of Receipt of Acceptance Improperly Dispatched

Where an acceptance is seasonably dispatched but the offeree uses means of transmission not invited by the offer or fails to exercise reasonable diligence to insure safe transmission, it is treated as operative upon dispatch if received within the time in which a properly dispatched acceptance would normally have arrived.

UCC

§ 2-204. Formation in General

(1) A contract for sale of goods may be made in any manner sufficient to show agreement, including offer and acceptance, conduct by both parties

which recognizes the existence of a contract, the interaction of electronic agents, and the interaction of an electronic agent and an individual.

(2) An agreement sufficient to constitute a contract for sale may be found even if the moment of its making is undetermined.

(3) Even if one or more terms are left open, a contract for sale does not fail for indefiniteness if the parties have intended to make a contract and there is a reasonably certain basis for giving an appropriate remedy.

(4)....

E. Allan Farnsworth
(opus cited p.114 et seq)

§ 3.6. Subjective and Objective Theories.

The subjectivists looked to the actual or subjective intentions of the parties. The subjectivists did not go so far as to advocate that subjective assent alone was *sufficient* to make a contract. Even under the subjective theory there had to be some manifestation of assent. But actual assent to the agreement on the part of both parties was *necessary*, and without it there could be no contract. In the much-abused metaphor, there had to be a "meeting of the minds."

The objectivists, on the other hand, looked to the external or objective appearance of the parties' intentions as manifested by their actions. One of the most influential objectivists, Judge Learned Hand, wrote in a memorable passage:

> A contract has, strictly speaking, nothing to do with the personal, or individual, intent of the parties. A contract is an obligation attached by the mere force of law to certain acts of the parties, usually words, which ordinarily accompany and represent a known intent. If, however, it were proved by twenty bishops that either party when he used the words intended something else than the usual meaning which the law imposes on them, he would still be held, unless there were mutual mistake or something else of the sort.

If one party's actions, judged by a standard of reasonableness, manifested to the other party an intention to agree, the real but unexpressed state of the first party's mind was irrelevant.

By the end of the nineteenth century, the objective theory had become ascendant and courts universally accept it today. In the words of a distinguished federal judge, "'intent' does not invite a tour through [plaintiff's] cranium, with [plaintiff] as the guide."

§ 3.22. Contracts by Correspondence.

It is more difficult to work out the mechanics of assent if the parties are at a distance and communicate by mail or some other means that takes time ...

The common law has tended ... to answer such questions without regard to reliance, on the simple assumption that there must be a single moment that is decisive in all cases—a moment after which the offeror's power to revoke is terminated, after which the offeree's power to reject is at an end, and after which any further risks of transmission are on the offeror.

The rule of *Adams v. Lindsell*, sometimes called the "mailbox rule," has met with general approval in the United States. Several explanations have been advanced. It has been argued that the offeror that makes an offer by mail authorizes the post office to receive the acceptance as the offeror's agent. It has also been argued that mailing the acceptance puts it irrevocably out of the offeree's control. A more convincing explanation is that the rule curtails the offeror's freedom to revoke by ending it at the earliest feasible time. Ending the offeror's power to revoke at the time of dispatch of the acceptance binds the offeror while the acceptance is in transit, even though the offeror does not know that the offer has been accepted and even though the offeree may not yet have relied on the contract ... The mailbox rule is extended to protect the offeree against termination by the offeror's death as well as by revocation.

As the master of the offer, the offeror can vary the mailbox rule by so providing. And even if the offer is silent, an acceptance is not effective on dispatch to terminate the offeror's power of revocation unless, as the Restatement Second puts it, it is "made in a manner and by a medium invited by" the offer. If the acceptance is not as invited, the rule does not apply, and the acceptance is not effective until receipt.

3. International/Multinational

CISG

Article 16

(1) Until a contract is concluded an offer may be revoked if the revocation reaches the offeree before he has dispatched an acceptance.

(2) However, an offer cannot be revoked:

(a) if it indicates, whether by stating a fixed time for acceptance or otherwise, that it is irrevocable; or

(b) if it was reasonable for the offeree to rely on the offer as being irrevocable and the offeree has acted in reliance on the offer.

Article 18

(1) [see supra p.59]

(2) An acceptance of an offer becomes effective at the moment the indication of assent reaches the offeror. An acceptance is not effective if the indication of assent does not reach the offeror within the time he has fixed or, if no time is fixed, within a reasonable time, due account being taken of the circumstances of the transaction, including the rapidity of the means of communication employed by the offeror. An oral offer must be accepted immediately unless the circumstances indicate otherwise.

(3) [see supra p.59]

Article 23

A contract is concluded at the moment when an acceptance of an offer becomes effective in accordance with the provisions of this Convention.

UNIDROIT

ARTICLE 2.1.3:
(*Withdrawal of offer*)

(1) An offer becomes effective when it reaches the offeree.

(2) An offer, even if it is irrevocable, may be withdrawn if the withdrawal reaches the offeree before or at the same time as the offer.

ARTICLE 2.1.4:
(*Revocation of offer*)

(1) Until a contract is concluded an offer may be revoked if the revocation reaches the offeree before it has dispatched an acceptance.

(2) However, an offer cannot be revoked

    (a) if it indicates, whether by stating a fixed time for acceptance or otherwise, that it is irrevocable; or

    (b) if it was reasonable for the offeree to rely on the offer as being irrevocable and the offeree has acted in reliance on the offer.

ARTICLE 2.1.6:
(*Mode of acceptance*)

(1) [see supra p.51]

(2) An acceptance of an offer becomes effective when the indication of assent reaches the offeror.

(3) [see supra p.51]

ARTICLE 2.1.9:
(*Late acceptance. Delay in transmission*)

(1) A late acceptance is nevertheless effective as an acceptance if without undue delay the offeror so informs the offeree or gives notice to that effect.

(2) If a communication containing a late acceptance shows that it has been sent in such circumstances that if its transmission had been normal it would have reached the offeror in due time, the late acceptance is effective as an acceptance unless, without undue delay, the offeror informs the offeree that it considers the offer as having lapsed.

Principles of European Contract Law

ARTICLE 1:303: NOTICE

(1) Any notice may be given by any means, whether in writing or otherwise, appropriate to the circumstances.

(2) Subject to paragraphs (4) and (5), any notice becomes effective when it reaches the addressee.

(3) A notice reaches the addressee when it is delivered to it or to its place of business or mailing address, or, if it does not have a place of business or mailing address, to its habitual residence.

...

(5) A notice has no effect if a withdrawal of it reaches the addressee before or at the same time as the notice.

(6) In this Article, 'notice' includes the communication of a promise, statement, offer, acceptance, demand, request or other declaration.

ARTICLE 2: 202: REVOCATION OF AN OFFER

(1) An offer may be revoked if the revocation reaches the offeree before it has dispatched its acceptance or, in cases of acceptance by conduct, before the contract has been concluded under Article 2:205(2) or (3).

(2) An offer made to the public can be revoked by the same means as were used to make the offer.

(3) However, a revocation of an offer is ineffective if:

    (a) the offer indicates that it is irrevocable; or

    (b) it states a fixed time for its acceptance; or

    (c) it was reasonable for the offeree to rely on the offer as being irrevocable and the offeree has acted in reliance on the offer.

C. Courts' Decisions

1. Civil Law Cases

Louisiana

Ever-Tite Roofing Corporation v. Green
83 So. 2d 449, 1956

AYRES, Judge.

Defendants executed and signed an instrument June 10, 1953, for the purpose of obtaining the services of plaintiff in re-roofing their residence [...] The document set out in detail the work to be done and the price [...] This instrument was likewise signed by plaintiff's sale representative, [...] this alleged contract contained these provisions:

'This agreement shall become binding only upon written acceptance hereof, by the principal or authorized officer of the Contractor, *or upon commencing performance of the work.* This contract is Not Subject to Cancellation. [...] Inasmuch as this work was to be performed entirely on credit, it was necessary for plaintiff to obtain credit reports and approval from the lending institution which was to finance said contract. [...] Additional information was requested by this situation, which was likewise in due course transmitted to the institution, which then gave its approval.

The day immediately following this approval, which was either June 18 or 19, plaintiff engaged its workmen and two trucks, loaded the trucks with the necessary roofing materials and proceeded [...] to defendants' residence for the purpose of doing the work [...] Upon their arrival at defendants' residence, the workmen found others in the performance of the work which plaintiff had contracted to do. Defendants notified plaintiff's workmen that the work had been contracted to other parties two days before and forbade them to do the work. [...]

The basis of the judgment appealed was that defendants had timely notified plaintiff before 'commencing performance of work.' The trial court held that notice to plaintiff's workmen upon their arrival with the materials that defendants did not desire them to commence the actual work was sufficient and timely to signify their intention to withdraw from the contract. With this conclusion we find ourselves unable to agree. [...]

The general rule of law is that an offer proposed may be withdrawn before its acceptance and that no obligation is incurred thereby. This is, however, not without exceptions. For instance, Restatement of the Law of Contracts stated:

'(1) The power to create a contract by acceptance of an offer terminates at the time specified in the offer, or, if no time is specified, at the end of a reasonable time.

'What is a reasonable time is a question of fact depending on the nature of the contract proposed, the usages of business and other circumstances of the case which the offeree at the time of his acceptance either knows or has reason to know.'

These principles are recognized in the Civil Code. LSA-C.C. Art. 1800 provides that an offer is incomplete as a contract until its acceptance and that before its acceptance the offer may be withdrawn. However, this general rule is modified by the provisions of LSA-C.C. Arts. 1801, 1802, 1804, and 1809 [...][24]

Therefore, since the contract did not specify the time within which it was to be accepted or within which the work was to have been commenced, a reasonable time must be allowed therefore in accordance with the facts and circumstances and the evident intention of the parties. [...] The delays to process defendants' application were not unusual. The contract was accepted by plaintiff by the commencement of the performance of the work contracted to be done. This commencement began with the loading of the trucks with the necessary materials [...] and transporting such materials and the workmen to defendants' residence. Actual commencement or performance of the work therefore began before any notice of dissent by defendants was given plaintiff. The proposition and its acceptance thus became a completed contract.

---

24. Former LSA-C.C. Art. 1802 is now Art. 1928 [see supra p.46].

Québec

Construction Polaris Inc. c.
Conseil de bande Micmacs de Gesgapegia
1997 WL 1930583 (C.Q.), J.E. 97-1341 (C.Q.)
Cour du Québec

Juge DENIS ROBERT.

[...]

3 According to the principles stated in articles 1378 et seq. of the Civil Code of Québec, one must not mix up a contract with the writing which incorporates its wording; the contract is the agreement between the parties and the writing is merely a means of proving the existence of the contract.

5 The acceptance by the defendants represents that moment when the contract was formed, ...

6 a. Art.1387: The contract is formed at that moment when the offeror receives the acceptance and where the acceptance is received, regardless of the method of communication used ...

Germany

BGH XII ZR 214/00, XII. Civil Senate, XII ZR 214/00
(engl. translation) in the web site of The University of Texas School of Law[25]

Facts:

By a lease in writing dated 23 March 1990 the defendant rented three warehouses from the claimant.... §2(2) of the lease provided that notice to terminate it as from 30 June or 31 December in any year must be given at least a year in advance. The parties further agreed that notice be by registered letter....

On 22 June 1995 the defendant wrote a letter terminating the lease as from 30 June 1996 and sent it to the claimant by Fax on 29 June. He added that the original would follow by hand the next day, and it was indeed placed in the claimant's letter-box about 10 a.m. on 30 June 1995. By then the claimant

---

25. http://www.utexas.edu/law/academics/centers/transnational/work/,[copyright holder].

and his wife had gone away on holiday. On 13 July 1995 the claimant wrote to the defendant stating that he had not received any proper notice of termination, and on 18 December 1995 he demanded rent from 1993 to 1995, alleged to be outstanding ... In his letter of reply on 19 December 1995 the defendant , as a precaution, gave notice of termination as from 31 December 1996, and on 30 June 1996 he vacated the premises....

The claimant sued for, inter alia, rent for the second half of 1996 and obtained from the Oberlandesgeright an increase in the sum awarded by the Landgericht, the court declaring that the lease had not been terminated until 31 December 1996, as per the defendant's notice of 19 December 1995.

The defendant's appeal succeeded:

Reasons:....

II.

1. The court below was correct to hold that the validity of the notice of termination did not depend on how it was communicated. §2(4) of the lease, which provided that notice must be in writing, and added that it be communicated by registered letter, made writing essential to the validity of the notice (§125(2) BGB) but it was only in order to ensure that the notice arrived that mention was made of registered letter. Notice of termination must normally be in writing to be valid, but its arrival need not be by registered letter. [references] The requirement of writing is met, as in this case, when a declaration of intention is sent by Fax.

2. The appellant is right to challenge the view of the court below that the Fax containing the defendant's declaration of intention to terminate the lease did not arrive on 29 June 1995. a) A declaration of intention addressed to a person not present is effective when it "arrives," and it arrives when it enters the addressee's zone of control, such that in normal circumstances he would be in a position to apprise himself of its contents. In principle declarations sent by teleprinter or Fax arrive when they are printed out by the addressee's printer, but arrival is never complete until the addressee is, or can in normal circumstances be expected to be, able to take note of it. Thus even in the case of a Fax message, the relevant time is when in accordance with normal practices the addressee could make himself aware of the contents.

b) On the findings of the court below the Fax message was printed out on the claimant's printer at 10.39 a.m. on 29 June 1995. The time of arrival is unaffected by the fact that at that moment the claimant was away on holiday. Contrary to the view of the court below, ability to apprise oneself of the message is to be understood objectively and in the abstract: it is not necessary that the recipient be actually aware of it. It is enough if the declaration of intention has entered the addressee's area of control so that in normal and unexceptional circumstances he could learn of it. To that extent the addressee is responsible for what happens in the area under his control. If he learns of a message which has entered his area of control only later or not at all, that is his problem. A declaration of intention may have "arrived" although the recipient is prevented from actually learning of its content whether by illness or, as in this case, by being away on holiday. It is for the recipient in such cases to take proper precautions, and if he fails to do so, arrival will not be prevented by such purely personal circumstances.

c) The respondent argues that the Fax message was merely an intimation that notice of termination was to follow. This is an error. It is clear from the note attached to the declaration of termination that the telefax itself constituted such a declaration. By sending the original as a follow-up the defendant was seeking to allay the notorious unreliability of telecommunications: whereas the Fax was sent in order to meet the time limit for the notice of termination the delivery of the original with its attendant receipt form was simply for purposes of evidence.

3. It is therefore not relevant whether the letter was placed in the claimant's mail-box in good time or not. Here the claimant had made a private arrangement with the postal authorities for his mail to be delivered between 8.30 and 9 a.m., but despite the contrary view of the court below such a private arrangement cannot affect the decision whether or not the letter arrived. According to the evidence, the letter was placed in the claimant's mail-box at about 10 a.m. on 30 June 1995, and if people generally would expect that at that time the mail-box was yet to be cleared, that is the day on which it arrived. A declaration placed in the addressee's mail-box after what people would expect to be the last collection is held not to have arrived, but whether that time has arrived or not depends not on the personal arrangements of the recipient, but rather, in the interests of legal certainty, on normal practice and expectation. According to the postal authorities, mail is generally delivered between 8.30 and 10.30 a.m. in the street where the claimant lives, so that objectively speaking one could expect that at 10 a.m. the mail-box was yet to be cleared.

The case must therefore be remanded to the court below for further proceedings and judgment.

2. Common Law Cases

U.K.

Carlill v. Carbolic Smoke Ball Company
[1893] 1 Q.B. 256

[Facts: The defendants, the proprietors of a medical preparation called "the Carbolic Smoke Ball," issued an advertisement in which they offered to pay 100*l.* to any person who contracted the influenza after having used one of their smoke balls in a specified manner and for a specified period. The plaintiff on the faith of the advertisement bought one of the balls, and used it in the manner and for the period specified, but nevertheless contracted the influenza]

LINDLEY, L.J.

[...]

We must first consider whether this was intended to be a promise at all, or whether it was a mere puff which meant nothing. Was it a mere puff? My answer to that question is No, and I base my answer upon this passage: "100*l.* is deposited with the Alliance Bank, shewing our sincerity in the matter." [...] The deposit is called in aid by the advertiser as proof of his sincerity of his promise to pay this 100*l.* in the event which he has specified. [...] there is the promise, as plain as words can make it.

Then it is contended that it is not binding. In the first place, it is said that it is not made with anybody in particular. [...] In point of law this advertisement is an offer to pay 100*l.* to anybody who will perform these conditions, and the performance of the conditions is the acceptance of the offer. [...] as a general proposition, when an offer is made, it is necessary in order to make a binding contract, not only that it should be accepted, but that the acceptance should be notified. [...] This offer is a continuing offer. It was never revoked, and if notice of acceptance is required [...] the person who makes the offer gets the notice of acceptance contemporaneously with his notice of the performance of the condition. [...] I [...] think that the true view, in a case of this kind, is that the person who makes the offer shews by his language and from the nature of the transaction that he does not expect and does not require notice of the acceptance apart from notice of the performance.

We, therefore, find here all the elements which are necessary to form a binding contract enforceable in point of law,[...] the true construction of this advertisement is that 100*l.* will be paid to anybody who uses this smoke ball three times daily for two weeks according to the printed directions, and who gets the influenza or cold or other diseases caused by taking cold within a reasonable time after so using it[...]

BOWEN, L.J.

[...]

It seems to me that in order to arrive at a right conclusion we must read this advertisement in its plain meaning, as the public would understand it. It was intended to be issued to the public and to be read by the public. How would an ordinary person reading this document construe it? It was intended unquestionably to have some effect, and I think the effect which it was intended to have, was to make people use the smoke ball as distinct from the purchase of it. [...] The intention was that the circulation of the smoke ball should be promoted, and that the use of it should be increased. [...]

Was it intended that the 100*l* should, if the conditions were fulfilled, be paid? The advertisement says that 100*l*. is lodged at the bank for the purpose. Therefore, it cannot be said that the statement that 100*l*. would be paid was intended to be a mere puff. [...]

It is not a contract made with all the world. There is the fallacy of the argument. It is an offer made to all the world;[...] It is an offer to become liable to any one who, before it is retracted, performs the condition, and, although the offer is made to the world, the contract is made with that limited portion of the public who come forward and perform the condition on the faith of the advertisement. [...] If this is an offer to be bound, then it is a contract the moment the person fulfils the condition.

Entores Ld. v. Miles Far East Corporation
[1955] 2 Q.B. 327

DENNING L.J.

[Facts: The plaintiffs are an English company. The defendants are an American corporation with agents all over the world, including a Dutch company in Amsterdam. The plaintiffs say that the contract was made by Telex between the Dutch company in Amsterdam and the English company in London. Communications by Telex are comparatively new. Each company has a teleprinter machine in its office; and each has a Telex number like a telephone number. When one company wishes to send a message to the other, it gets the Post Office to connect up the machines. Then a clerk at one end taps the message on to his machine just as if it were a typewriter, and it is instantaneously passed to the machine at the other end, which automatically types the message onto paper at that end.]

[...]

The offer was sent by Telex from England offering to pay £239 10s. a ton for 100 tons, and accepted by Telex from Holland. [...]

When a contract is made by post it is clear law throughout the common law countries that the acceptance is complete as soon as the letter is put into the post box, and that is the place where the contract is made. But there is no clear rule about the contracts made by telephone or by Telex. Communications by these means are virtually instantaneous and stand on a different footing.[...]

My conclusion is, that the rule about instantaneous communications between the parties is different from the rule about the post. The contract is only complete when the acceptance is received by the offeror: and the contract is made at the place where the acceptance is received.

In a matter of this kind, however, it is very important that the countries of the world should have the same rule. I find that most of the European countries have substantially the same rule as that I have stated. Indeed, they apply it to contracts by post as well as instantaneous communications. But in the United States of America it appears as if instantaneous communications are treated in the same was as postal communications.[...]

PARKER L.J.

[...]the requirement as to actual notification of the acceptance is for the benefit of the offeror, he may waive it and agree to the substitution for that requirement of some other conduct by the acceptor. He may do so expressly, as in the advertisement cases, by intimating that he is content with the performance of a condition. Again, he may do so impliedly by indicating a contemplated method of acceptance, for example, by post or telegram.[...]

So far as Telex messages are concerned, [...] I can see no reason for departing from the general rule that there is no binding contract until notice of the acceptance is received by the offeror.

U.S.A.

Rhode Island Tool Company v. United States
130 Ct. Cl. 698, 1128 F. Supp. 417, 1955.

JONES, Chief Judge.

[...]

On September 10, 1948, in response to an invitation to bid, plaintiff submitted a bid on a number of items contained in the invitation[...]

The sales manager of the plaintiff who prepared its bid failed to notice the change in the description of the bolts from stud to machine on the third page and calculated plaintiff's bid on the basis of stud bolts. The machine bolts were a more expensive type of bolt. [...]

Notice of award to plaintiff was mailed on October 4, 1948. [...]

The plaintiff discovered its error late on Friday afternoon, October 1, and on the first working day thereafter, Monday, October 4, 1948, plaintiff's sales manager communicated with plaintiff's representative in Philadelphia, who immediately telephoned the Aviation Supply Office of the Navy Department in Philadelphia, notifying that office of plaintiff's error and that it desired to withdraw its bid [...] The record does not show whether the notice of award was mailed before or after the telephone conversation in which plaintiff advised the defendant of its mistake and asked to withdraw its bid. It was received by plaintiff after the telegram of withdrawal had been sent.[...]

The question is whether, in all the circumstances of this case, the depositing of the notice of award in the mail constitutes a binding contract from which plaintiff cannot escape, notwithstanding the mistake was brought to the attention of the contracting officials before the notice of award was received.

We believe that when the record is considered as a whole in the light of modern authorities, there was no binding contract, since plaintiff withdrew its bid before the acceptance became effective.

Under the old post office regulations when a letter was deposited in the mail the sender lost all control of it. It was irrevocably on its way. After its deposit in the mail the post office became, in effect, the agent of the addressee. Naturally the authorities held that the acceptance in any contract became final when it was deposited in the post office, since the sender had lost control of the letter at that time. That was the final act in consummating the agreement.

But some years ago the united States Postal authorities completely changed the regulation. It read as follows in 1948:

'Withdrawal by sender before dispatch. (a) After mail matter has been deposited in a post office it shall not be withdrawn except by the sender, 'Recall of matter after dispatch. (a) When the sender of any article of unregistered mail matter desires its return after it has been dispatched from the mailing office application shall be made to the postmaster at the office of mailing.[...]

When this new regulation became effective, the entire picture was changed. The sender now does not lose control of the letter the moment it is deposited in the post office, but retains the right of control up to the time of delivery. The acceptance, therefore, is not final until the latter reaches destination, since the sender has the absolute right of withdrawal from the post office, and even the right to have the postmaster at the delivery point return the letter at any time before actual delivery. [...]

We know of no decision of any court to the contrary since the effective date of the new regulation, where the new regulation was called to the attention of the court. The English courts have construed a similar regulation to mean finality at point of destination and courts in this country have so construed the regulation.

Chapter Five

Cause and Consideration

Besides offer and acceptance, among the other legal requirements which are necessary, in both the civil law and the common law traditions, to make a contract binding and create obligations, is the requirement of "cause" at civil law and the requirement of "consideration" at common law. In this latter legal system, the existence of "some" consideration is a required element for the validity of all contracts (except those contracts made under seal) meant to be binding, whereas at civil law there must exist a lawful "cause" or lawful reason to make a promise by one party binding on that party or on both parties depending on the nature of the juridical act entered into.[26]

A: Civil Law Systems

La. Civ. C

Art. 1966 "An obligation cannot exist without a lawful cause."

Art. 1967-1 "Cause is the reason why a party obligates himself"

Art. 1969 "An obligation may be valid even though its cause is not expressed"

Fr. Civ. C.

Art. 1108 "Four requirements are essential for the validity of a convention:

-consent of the party who binds herself;

-capacity to contract;

-an object which is the matter of the commitment;

-a cause which justifies the commitment"

Art. 1131 "An obligation without a cause, or based on a false cause, or on an illicit cause, can have no effects."

---

26. unilateral v. bilateral: see supra p.13 et seq.

Art. 1132 "The convention is valid although its cause is not expressly stated."

C.C.Q.

Art. 1410 "The cause of a contract is the reason that determines each of the parties to enter into the contract.

The cause need not be expressed."

Art. 1141 "A contract whose cause is prohibited by law or contrary to public order is null"

It. Civ. C.

Art. 1325 Indication of requisites. The requisites of the contract are:

1) agreement of the parties (1326 *ff.*);

2) *causa* (1343 *ff.*);

3) object (1346 *ff.*);

4) form, when prescribed by law, under penalty of nullity (1350 *ff.*).

Art. 1343 Unlawful causa. The *causa* is unlawful when it is contrary to mandatory rules, public policy, or morals (1344, 1418).

Art. 1345 Unlawful motive. A contract is unlawful when the parties are led to conclude it solely by an unlawful motive, common to both.

Distinguishing itself, in this respect, from both the civil law and the common law systems, German law does not refer to an objective theory of "cause" and it does not require "consideration" as a necessary requirement for a contract. German law will use other legal devices or instruments [such as a lack of seriousness of the declaration of intent: BGB § 118] to achieve the same results as are achieved by "cause" and "consideration." In the area of "Unjust Enrichment" [Title 26 of the B.G.B.] it is possible to identify an implicit reference to the concept of "cause" under the guise of "without legal grounds":

BGB

§ 812 Principle

(1) Anyone gaining something through another party's efforts or otherwise at his expense without legal grounds for doing so is under a duty to make restitution to him. This duty also obtains if the legal grounds later lapse or if the results intended with those efforts according to the contents of the legal transaction do not occur.

(2) Efforts also include acknowledgement of the existence or non-existence of a debt relationship.

Sw. Fed. C.O.

Art 17 "An acknowledgment of debt shall be valid even without expressing the legal ground thereof."

Art. 62 "Any person who has in an unjustifiable manner received a gain out of the property of another is bound to return it.

The gain must in particular be returned, where it was received without any valid ground or on a ground which did not become effective or which ceased to exist."

Planiol et Ripert, Treatise on the Civil Law Vol. 2 Part 1
by 11th ed. 1939 (translated by the Louisiana State Law Institute 1959)

§ 2. Origin of The Theory of Cause

1029. Its creation by Domat
Domat was the creator of the theory of cause. Before him Dumoulin and B. d'Argentré did not know of it, and the more ancient Customs which sometimes speak of cause use the word in quite a different sense.

1030. Analysis of the Ideas of Domat
In the first place, the theory of cause is founded on the three essential ideas of which it is composed:

(1) In synallagmatic contracts, the obligation of each of the two parties has as cause the engagement undertaken by the other. The two obligations mutually sustain each other and serve, as Domat says, as the "foundation" of the other.

(2) In "real" contracts, such as loan, where there is only a single obligation, such obligation is created by the giving of the thing. It is this "giving" which "forms" the obligation, which is the "foundation" of it, or the "cause."

(3) In gratuitous contracts, where there is neither reciprocity of obligations, nor prior performances, the "cause" of the obligation of the donor can only be found in the motives of liberal intention, that is to say in the dominating reason which has pushed the author of the

donation to consent. This is what Domat did, and it is impossible to find anything else which can serve as cause for the promise to give.

1031. Roman Origin of the Ideas of Domat

Domat found in the Roman law the elements of his theory of cause, and he himself indicates in a note the texts he made use of.[.... ..]

1032. Incorporation of the Ideas of Domat in the Code

Since Domat, the theory of cause has not changed. Pothier, notably, only reproduced the ideas of his predecessor: "Every obligation must have an honest cause. If the cause does exist, if it is false, or if it offends good morals, the obligation is null, as well as the contract which includes it" (...). As to the definition of cause, Pothier repeats the passage of "Loix Civiles" ..."In business contracts, the cause of the engagement of one of the parties is what the other party gives him, or engages to give him ... In the contracts of benevolence, the liberality which one of the parties wishes to show to the other is a cause sufficient for the engagement." The articles of the Code were inspired by those passages of Pothier, and thus are traceable to Domat through Pothier as his intermediary.

1036B. Search for Distinction Between Cause and Motive

Modern authors who have studied the theory of cause are especially attached to this distinction, M. Capitant (...), sees as the cause the purpose of the contract which forms an integral part of the manifestation of will creating the obligation, while the motive is the contingent reason and personal to each contractor. A motive becomes the cause of the contract when it constitutes for the two parties the determining reason of their accord. This idea that the cause is the purpose pursued by the parties was accepted with some modifications in several modern studies of cause (...). It encounters, however, serious objections. To distinguish the purpose from the motive, one is forced to say that the purpose pursued is the motive which for the two parties is the determining reason for their accord. In reality the motives are always personal to each one of the parties, there may be reciprocal knowledge by each party of the motives which induce the other contractant to act, but there is never a common end.(...).

§4. Criticism of the Theory of Cause

1037. Its Fundamental Vices

The theory of cause, such as French doctrine has construed it, has two defects: (1) it is false, at least in two cases out of three; (2) it is useless.

1038. Falsity of the Notion of Cause

1039. Uselessness of Notion of Cause

1039A. Actual Practical Value of the Theory of Cause

If this theory of cause has not been abandoned, it is because in reality, the notion of cause has given the jurisprudence precious support for the annulling of acts, on an onerous or gratuitous title, which are dictated by an illicit or immoral motive. Art. 6 of the Civil Code would have sufficed, but when the contract is contrary to public order by the motives which inspire it and not by its object, the jurisprudence makes use of Art. 1133. The theory of cause is thus the object of innumerable applications, but only in so far as it concerns the annulment of juridical acts (...).

Philippe Malaurie, Laurent Aynès, Philippe Stoffel-Munck
Les Obligations, Defrénois 2003

603. Justification, limitation and guarantee. — 'The cause' is, at the same time, the justification, the limitation and the guarantee of the autonomous power of the will. It is its justification by explaining why the will can bind: it is not enough to say that one is committed because one wants to be bound, it is also necessary to know 'why.' It is also its limitation: an obligation, albeit wanted, is not binding, if it is without a cause or is grounded on an illicit cause (art. 1133). It is, finally, its guarantee because to deprive a will of its effects a judge is not free to make up his mind as regards the motives which have enticed a person to bind herself.

B. Common Law Systems: Consideration

1. English Common Law

Blackstone; Commentaries: Book II the Rights of Things
Ch. 30. p.443–445

Having thus shown the general nature of a contract, we are, secondly, to proceed to the *consideration* upon which it is founded; or the reason which moves the party contracting to enter into the contract. "It is an agreement, upon *sufficient consideration*." The civilians hold, that in all contracts, either express or implied there must be something given in exchange, something that is mutual or reciprocal. This thing, which is the price or motive of the contract, we call the consideration: and it must be a thing lawful in itself, or else the contract is void. A *good* consideration [...] is that of blood or natural affection between near relations; the satisfaction accruing from which the law esteems an equivalent for whatever benefit may move from one relation to another. This consideration may sometimes however be set aside, and the contract become void, when it tends in it's consequences to defraud creditors or other third persons of their just rights. But a contract for *any valuable* consideration, as for marriage, for money, for work done, or for other reciprocal contracts, can never be impeached at law; and, if it be of a sufficient adequate value, is never set aside in equity: for the person contracted with has then given an equivalent in recompense, and is therefore as much an owner, or a creditor, as any other person.[...]

A CONSIDERATION of some sort or other is so absolutely necessary to the forming of a contract, that a *nudum pactum* or agreement to do or pay any thing on one side, without any compensation on the other, is totally void in law; and a man cannot be compelled to perform it. As if one man promises to give another 100 *l.* here there is nothing contracted for or given on the one side, and therefore, there is nothing binding on the other.[....]

P.S. Atiyah

(opus cited)

I. the nature of the Doctrine of Consideration (at p.124 et seq.)

[...] the doctrine of consideration has traditionally rested on two main legs. The first of these is the idea that a promise is legally binding if it is given in return for some benefit which is rendered, or to be rendered, to the promisor. The second is the notion that a promise becomes binding if the promise incurs a detriment by reliance upon it, that is, if he changes his position in reliance on the promise in such a way that he would be worse off if the promise is broken than he would have been if the promise had never been made at all.[...]

There are many circumstances in which those who receive benefits at the hands of others may be compelled to pay for them even if no promise has been given at all. Sometimes we explain such cases by arguing that they are cases of implied promises. But there is also a large body of law—known formerly as the law of quasi-contract, and today as the law of restitution— which is concerned with cases where a person is liable to pay for benefits obtained even if there is nothing that could be remotely called an implied promise. [...]

Similarly, the other leg of the doctrine of consideration has close connections with other branches of the law, such as the law of torts, and also various equitable doctrines, as well as the doctrine of 'estoppel' in its various forms.[...]

G.H. Treitel

(opus cited)

In English law, a promise is not, as a general rule, binding as a contract unless it is either made under seal or supported by some "consideration." The purpose of the doctrine of consideration is to put some legal limits on the enforceability of agreements even where they are intended to be legally binding and are not vitiated by some factor such as mistake, misrepresentation, duress, or illegality.[...].

The basic feature of that doctrine is the idea of reciprocity: something of value in the eye of the law" must be given for a promise in order to make it enforceable as a contract. An informal gratuitous promise therefore does not amount to a contract. A person or body to whom a promise of a gift is made from purely charitable or sentimental motives gives nothing for the promise; and the claims of such a promise are obviously less compelling than those of a person who has given (or promised) some return for the promise. The invalidity of informal gratuitous promises of this kind can also be supported on the ground that their enforcement could prejudice third parties such as creditors of the promisor. Such promises, too, may be rashly made; and the requirements of executing a deed or giving value provide at least some protection against this danger.

The doctrine of consideration, however, also strikes at many promises which are not "gratuitous" in any ordinary or commercial sense. These applications of the doctrine can be brought within its scope by stressing that consideration must be not merely "something of value," but "something of value *in the eye of the law.*" [...]

1. Consideration need not be Adequate

Under the doctrine of consideration the courts will not enforce a promise unless some value has been given for it. But they do not, in general, ask whether adequate value has been given, or whether the agreement is harsh or one-sided. The reason for this is not that the courts cannot value the promise of each party: they have to do just this when assessing damages. It is rather that they should not interfere with the bargain actually made by the parties. The fact that a person pays "too much" or "too little" for a thing may be evidence of fraud or mistake, or it may induce the court to imply a warranty or to hold that a contract has been frustrated. But it does not of itself affect the validity of the contract.[....]

2. Nominal Consideration

(1) Sufficiency of nominal consideration

Where an agreement is legally binding on the ground that it is supported by nominal consideration, the doctrine of consideration does not, of course, serve its main purpose, of distinguishing between gratuitous and onerous promises. But the law has no settled policy against enforcing all gratuitous promises. It only refuses to enforce *informal* gratuitous promises; and the deliberate use of a nominal consideration can be regarded as a form to make a gratuitous promise binding.[...]

(2) Nominal and inadequate consideration

It is not normally necessary to distinguish between "nominal" and "inadequate" consideration, since both equally suffice to make a promise binding. The need to draw the distinction may, however, arise in some of the exceptional cases in which the law treats promises or transfers supported only by nominal consideration differently from those supported by substantial or "valuable" consideration (even though it may be inadequate).[...]

2. Past Acts or Promises requested by Promisor

Even an act done before a promise was made can be consideration for it if three conditions are satisfied: the act must have been done at the request of the promisor; it must have been understood that payment would be made; and the payment, if it had been promised in advance, must have been legally recoverable.[...]

SECTION 4. CONSIDERATION MUST MOVE FROM THE PROMISEE

The rule that consideration "must move from the promisee" means that a person to whom a promise was made can only enforce it if he himself provided the consideration for it. He cannot sue if the consideration for the promise moved from a third party.[...]

SECTION 5. CONSIDERATION MUST BE OF SOME VALUE

1. Must be of Economic Value

An act, omission or promise will only amount to consideration if the law recognizes that it has some economic value. It may have such value even though the value cannot be precisely quantified. But "natural affection of itself is not a sufficient consideration," and the same is true of other merely sentimental motives for promising.[...]

3. Trivial Acts

Since consideration need not be adequate, acts or omissions of very small value can be consideration.[...]

4. Gift of Onerous Property

A promise to give away onerous property is binding if the donee promises in return to discharge obligations attached to it.[...]

5. Compromise and Forbearance to Sue

A promise not to enforce a valid claim is clearly good consideration for a promise given in return.[...]

2. United States Common Law

Restatement, 2d

Chapter 4 Formation of Contracts-Consideration

Topic 1. The Requirement of Consideration

§71. Requirement of Exchange: Types of Exchange

(1) To constitute consideration, a performance or a return promise must be bargained for.

(2) A performance or return promise is bargained for if it is sought by the promisor in exchange for his promise and is given by the promisee in exchange for that promise.

(3) The performance may consist of (a) an act other than a promise, or (b) a forbearance, or (c) the creation, modification, or destruction of a legal relation.

(4) The performance or return promise may be given to the promisor or to some other person. It may be given by the promisee or by some other person.

§72 Exchange of Promise for Performance

Except as stated in §§73 and 74, any performance which is bargained for is consideration.

§73 Performance of Legal Duty

Performance of a legal duty owed to a promisor which is neither doubtful nor the subject of honest dispute is not consideration; but a similar performance is consideration if it differs from what was required by the duty in a way which reflects more than a pretense of bargain.

§79 Adequacy of Consideration: Mutuality of Obligation

If the requirement of consideration is met, there is no additional requirement of (a) a gain, advantage, or benefit to the promisor or a loss, disadvantage, or detriment to the promisee; or (b) equivalence in the values exchanged; or (c) "mutuality of obligation."

UCC

§2-205. Firm Offers

An offer by a merchant to buy or sell goods in a signed writing which by its terms gives assurance that it will be held open is not revocable, for lack of consideration, during the time stated or if no time is stated for a reasonable time, but in no event may such period of irrevocability exceed three months; but any such term of assurance on a form supplied by the offeree must be separately signed by the offeror.

§2-209 Modification, Rescission and Waiver

(1) An agreement modifying a contract within this Article needs no consideration to be binding.

(2) –(5)

O.W. Holmes, Jr., The Common Law
1881

(p.253) Our law does not enforce every promise which a man may make. Promises made as ninety-nine promises out of a hundred are, by word of mouth or simple writing, are not binding unless there is a consideration for them. That is, as it is commonly explained, unless the promisee has either conferred a benefit on the promisor, or incurred a detriment, as the inducement to the promise.

It has been thought that this rule was borrowed from the Roman law by the Chancery, and, after undergoing some modification there, passed into the common law.

But this account of the matter is at least questionable.

(p.269 et seq) Moreover, before consideration was ever heard of, debt was the time-honored remedy on every obligation to pay money enforced by law, except the liability to damages for a wrong ...

To sum up, the action of debt has passed through three stages. At first, it was the only remedy to recover money due, except when the liability was simply to pay damages for a wrongful act.... .

The second stage was when the doctrine of consideration was introduced in its earlier form of a benefit to the promisor. This applied to all contracts not under seal while it prevailed, but it was established while debt was the only action for money payable by such contracts.

The third stage was reached when a larger view was taken of consideration, and it was expressed in terms of detriment to the promisee.

(p.293–4) It is said that consideration must not be confounded with motive. It is true that it must not be confounded with what may be the prevailing or chief motive in actual fact. A man may promise to paint a picture for five hundred dollars, while his chief motive may be a desire for fame. A consideration may be given and accepted, in fact, solely for the purpose of making a promise binding. But, nevertheless, it is the essence of a consideration, that, by the terms of the agreement, it is given and accepted as the motive or inducement of the promise. Conversely, the promise must be made and accepted as the conventional motive or inducement for furnishing the consideration. The root of the whole matter is the relation of reciprocal conventional inducement, each for the other, between consideration and promise

E. Allan Farnsworth

(opus cited)

§ 1.6. The Development of a General Basis for Enforcing Promises. [...] During the sixteenth century, the word *consideration*, which had earlier been used without technical significance, came to be used as a word of art to express the sum of the conditions necessary for an action in assumpsit to lie. It was therefore a tautology that a promise, at least if not under seal, was enforceable only if there was *consideration*, for this was to say no more than that it was enforceable only under those circumstances in which the action of assumpsit was allowed. In this way, however, the word *consideration* came to be applied to the test of enforceability of a promise and to be used to distinguish those promises that in the eyes of the common law where of sufficient significance to society to justify the legal sanctions of assumpsit for their enforcement.

It was, not surprisingly, neither a simple nor a logical test. Bound up in it were several elements. Most importantly, from the *quid pro quo* of debt, by way of the later extension of general assumpsit, came the notion that there must be a benefit to the promisor. From the reliance of special assumpsit came the notion that there must be a detriment to the promisee.

The requirement of such an exchange found easy acceptance in a society entering a commercial age. The doctrine of consideration took care of the bulk of economically vital commercial agreements, even if it afforded no ground for the enforceability of gratuitous promises, for which nothing was given in exchange.[...]

As a cornerstone for the law of contract, the doctrine of consideration has been widely criticized. It would be foolhardy to attempt to defend it by an exercise in logic, for it must be viewed in the light of its history and of the society that produced it. Nevertheless, in view of the difficulty that other societies have had in developing a general basis for enforcing promises, it is perhaps less remarkable that the basis developed by the common law is logically flawed than that the common law succeeded in developing any basis at all.

§ 2.2. The Bargain Test of Consideration. Among the limitations on the enforcement of promises, the most fundamental is the requirement of consideration. For a time during the nineteenth century a "will theory," under which a promise was enforceable because the promisor had "willed" to be bound by the promise, was prevalent. But that notion was to give way to one based on bargain.[...] By the end of the nineteenth century, at least in the United States, the traditional requirement that the consideration be either a benefit to the promisor or a detriment to the promise had begun to be replaced by a requirement that the consideration be "bargained for."[...].

§ 2.3. **What Can Constitute Consideration.** Virtually anything that anyone would bargain for in exchange for a promise can be consideration for that promise. The same consideration can support a number of promises. Furthermore, as long as part of what is given in exchange for a promise is consideration it is immaterial that the rest is not.[...]

§ 2.8. **Moral Obligation.** By the latter half of the sixteenth century, courts had accepted the general principle that "past consideration" could not be consideration. There was, however, pressure to allow exception for promises to perform what could be regarded as a "moral obligation." One such situation arose if a debtor promised to pay a debt that had been barred by the statute of limitations. Although no longer under a legal obligation to pay the debt, the debtor might be thought to have a moral obligation to do so. [...] Although judges may speak of "past consideration" or of "moral obligation" as consideration, they are really making an exception to the requirement of a bargained-for exchange. Such promises as fall within that exception are simply enforceable without consideration, at least as that term is understood under the bargain test.[...]

§ 2.11. **Peppercorns and Pretense of Bargain.** [...] To be practical, then, we must restate the example in this way: a donor promises to make a gift of a farm to a donee, and, in order to make the promise enforceable, the donee gives a dollar to the donor. Is the donor's promise supported by consideration? There is some authority, including the first Restatement, that it is, at least if the transaction is cast in the form of a bargain. The more modern view, however, mirrored in the Restatement Second, requires an actual bargain, not merely a pretense of bargain, and such extreme disparity in the exchange as here supposed would reveal the purported bargain to be a sham. Under this view the donor's promise is not supported by consideration.

C. Courts' Decisions

1. Civil Law Cases

France

Cour de Cassation (Ch.civ., 1re sect.)
18 avril 1953
Gaz.Pal. 1953.2.7.

[Facts: Doctor M ... died on Sept.8, 1944. A genealogist, B ... was asked by the notary of the Doctor's family to locate the 'female' heir of the deceased. On Nov.26,1944, B ... made Ms P.., the deceased's niece and sole heir, to sign a contract whereby he would disclose to her the inheritance she was to receive if she paid him a substantial percentage of the inheritance. After the signature of the contract, B ... disclosed to Ms P ... that she was Doctor M ...'s niece and his sole heir.]

The Court:

The appeal claims that the Court of Appeal was wrong in ruling, at the request of the spouses P..., that the contract was null for lack of cause when Ms P ... had been running the risk of not knowing about her inheritance and that without the involvement of the genealogist it would have been impossible to discover her name and her address. But, considering that on the basis of its own holdings and those of the lower court's judgment, the Court of Appeal's decision, on the basis of the documents in this case and the results of the investigation, properly observed that Ms P ...'s address was known by the people surrounding the Doctor as well as by the notary; considering that the latter, too hastily and without beforehand consulting the documents and archives in his hands, had uselessly instructed B ... to undertake an investigation, and had given him all the necessary information to definitely locate Ms P ... ; considering that B ... had not rendered any service whatsoever to Ms P ... ; that the existence of the succession would have quite normally come to the attention of the heir without any intervention on the part of the genealogist; on the basis of these observations, the Court of Appeal could reach the conclusion that there had been no disclosure of any secret and that the contract of Nov.26, 1944 was without a cause; hence, the Court could hold the contract null ...

Louisiana
Davis-Delcambre Motors, Inc. v. Martin Simon
154 So. 2d 775, La. App. 1963

FRUGE, Judge.

The plaintiff Davis-Delcambre Motors, Inc., sued the defendant, Martin Simon, on his promissory note dated June 14, 1957 in the amount of $300.00. Defendant, by special plea, raised the defense of illegal consideration as a bar to collection on the note.[...]

... during the first week of June 1957, Wilmer Mitchel purchased a 1952 Chevrolet automobile from the plaintiff. [...] Mitchel gave plaintiff two checks, in the amounts of $200 and $100 [...] Plaintiff attempted to cash these checks at the named bank but was informed that Wilmer Mitchel had no account. Accordingly, payment was refused. About one week later plaintiff contacted Wilmer Mitchel and threatened to have him arrested for issuing worthless checks. Subsequently Martin Simon, Michel's employer, issued a promissory note in the exact amount of the worthless checks. [...]

Counsel for defendant argues that the consideration for the note at issue was the debt of Wilmer Mitchel, and that the payment of a debt of a third person is valid consideration. In our opinion, counsel has correctly stated the law in this regard. [...] However, viewing the evidence and testimony as a whole we are convinced that the payment of the debt of Wilmer Mitchel was not the cause which motivated defendant to make the note.[...]

All contracts which have as their object that which is forbidden by law or contrary to good morals are void. LSA-C.C. Art. 1892. By the 'cause' of a contract is meant the motive or consideration for making it. LSA-C.C. Art. 1896. 'The cause is unlawful, when it is forbidden by law, when it is contra bonos mores (contrary to moral conduct) or to public order.' LSA-C.C. Art. 1895. Accordingly, it has been held that the promise of a father to pay the debt of his insolvent son in exchange for the creditor's promise not to prosecute for fraud is without a good consideration and void, as against public policy. [...] Similarly, the courts have refused to enforce promises to pay gambling debts. [...] the obvious consideration for the note in question was the forbearance to prosecute Mitchel for issuing a worthless check. [...] In our opinion, it is axiomatic that the promise to suppress the prosecution of this crime is Contra bonos mores and results in rendering the note sued upon void for lack of consideration. [...] For the reasons assigned, the judgment of the lower court is reversed and plaintiff's suit is dismissed[...]

Québec

James Hutchison v. The Royal Institution
for the Advancement of Learning

1932 Canada Law Reports, Supreme Court of Canada,
[1932] S.C.R. p.57

[Facts: In March, 1914, R. offered to give to McGill University, namely the respondent, $150,000 for the erection and equipment of a gymnasium and the offer was accepted; but the building was deferred owing to the war. In 1920, the university authorities undertook a campaign for a "Centennial Endowment Fund" and R., by the terms of a "Subscription and Pledge Card," then promised to contribute $200,000 to that fund on the condition that the previous offer of $150,000 would be included in the subsequent offer, the university being at the same time released from the obligation of erecting the gymnasium. R. paid $100,000 dated December 1, 1925, and payable three years after date. R. became insolvent and the trustee in bankruptcy disallowed the respondent's claim for the amount of the note and the interest accrued.[...]]

ANGLIN, C.J.C.

[...]the proposition seems to me so clear that it can require no citation of authority to support it, that, whether the matter be dealt with under the law of England, or under R.S.C. 1927, c. 16, s. 53, the extension of time for payment of the $200,000 was a "valuable" consideration for the giving by Mr. Ross of the note in question.

The only question, therefore, requiring further discussion here seems to be whether or not Ross did incur a legally enforceable obligation to pay $200,000 towards the endowment fund of the university. That question, it seems to me, must be determined according to the law of the province of Québec, where the contract to pay was entered into, and was intended to be carried out, and, if need be, enforced. According to that law there can be no question that there had been a real and lawful "cause" (Arts. 982, 984, 1131, C.C.) for Mr. Ross's promise to pay $150,000, to be used towards the cost of the erection of a gymnasium, to be known as the Ross Memorial Gymnasium. It follows that the release of that obligation afforded a like lawful "cause" for the promise to pay the $200,000.

NEWCOMBE J.

[...] It is true that the rules of the common law of England, including the law merchant, apply to bills of exchange and promissory notes, because the Parliament of Canada has, [...] so declared in the exercise of its exclusive legislative authority over that subject; but the Dominion legislation does not and was not intended to affect a subscriber's liability to implement his subscription, and, as I understood the argument, no contention to the contrary was submitted.

I quote articles 982 and 984 of the Civil Code of Québec:

982. It is essential to an obligation that it should have a cause from which it arises, persons between whom it exists, and an object.

984. there are four requisites to the validity of a contract: [...]

A lawful cause of consideration.

It is essential therefore that an obligation shall have "a cause from which it arises," and that a contract shall have "a lawful cause or consideration"; but it is not meant that a contract which has a lawful cause within the meaning of article 984 C.C. shall be void or defective for lack of that which, under the English authorities, would constitute valuable consideration.

Article 1131 of the *Code Civil* provides that

1131. L'obligation sans cause, ou sur une fausse cause, ou sur une cause illicite, ne peut avoir aucun effet.

[...]

I extract the following paragraph from Sir Frederick Pollock's Principles of Contract at p.185.

No one ever argued before an English temporal court that deliberate bounty or charitable intention will support a formless promise; but such was undoubtedly the canonical view, and is to this day, in theory, the rule of legal systems which have followed the modern Roman law. There was no room within the common law scheme of actions for turning natural into legal obligation.

[...]

My interpretation of the authorities, as applicable to the facts of this case, leads me to the view that there were both lawful cause and consideration for Mr. Ross's subscription, within the meaning of the Civil Code of Québec; and that, as to the note, by the giving of which Mr. Ross, at his urgent request, secured an extension of the time limited for the payment of the balance of his subscription, the consideration was valuable and satisfied the requirements of the common law and of the *Bills of Exchange Act*.[...]

2. Common Law Cases

U.K.

Esso Petroleum Co. Ltd v. Customs and Excise Commissioners
[1976] 1 W.L.R. 1

[Facts: The plaintiffs ("Esso"), suppliers of and dealers in petrol, commissioned the manufacture of coins bearing on one side the head of one of the 30 English footballers chosen for the 1970 World Cup competition and on the other the word "Esso." To promote sales the coins were, as advertised, distributed free to any motorist buying petrol from Esso filling stations and dealers on the basis of one coin for every four gallons of petrol purchased. The Customs and Excise Commissioners claimed that the coins were goods chargeable to purchase tax […] as being "produced in quantity for general sale," and claimed tax accordingly.]

VISCOUNT DILHORNE.

[…] that the coins were produced in quantity and for general distribution is clear and not disputed. Were they produced for sale?[…] The question to be decided is, were they sold or intended to be sold by the garage proprietors to purchasers of petrol? […]

The respondents' intention was to promote the sale of their petrol by tempting persons to buy petrol from their dealers in the hope of securing a complete set of coins[…]

They sent each of their dealers who participated in the campaign a pamphlet telling him to give one coin to each customer buying four gallons; two coins if eight gallons were bought and so on. […]

If the coins were a free gift to every customer who purchased four gallons of petrol or multiples of that quantity, then the appeal must be dismissed. If, on the other hand, a legal contract was entered into between the customer and the dealer which, in addition to the supply of petrol, involved the dealer in a legally binding obligation to transfer a coin or coins to the customer, and if that legal contract amounted to a sale, then the appeal must be allowed.

Was there any intention on the part of the garage proprietor and also on the part of the customer who bought four gallons, or multiples of that quantity, of petrol to enter into a legally binding contract in relation to a coin or coins?[…]

If a coin was just to be given to the motorist, it would not be necessary for there to have been any agreement between him and the garage proprietor with regard to it. [...]

I see no reason to imply any intention to enter into contractual relations from the statements on the posters that a coin would be given if four gallons of petrol were bought. [...]

If, however, there was any contract relating to the coin or coins, the consideration for the entry into that contract was not the payment of any money but the entry into a contract to purchase four gallons or multiples of that quantity of petrol, in which case the contract relating to the coin or coins cannot be regarded as a contract of sale.[...]

LORD SIMON OF GLAISDALE.

[...]

The coins may have been themselves of little intrinsic value; but all the evidence suggests that Esso contemplated that they would be attractive to motorists and that there would be a large commercial advantage to themselves from the scheme, an advantage to which the garage proprietors also would share.[...]

What the garage proprietor says by his placards is in fact and in law and offer of consideration to the motorist to enter into a contract of sale of petrol [...] the motorist who does notice the placard, and in reliance thereon drives in and orders the petrol, is in law doing two things at the same time. First, he is accepting the offer of a coin if he buys four gallons of petrol. Secondly, he is himself offering to buy four gallons of petrol: this offer is accepted by the filling of his tank. [...]

Here the coins were not transferred for a money consideration. They were transferred in consideration of the motorist entering into a contract for the sale of petrol. The coins were therefore not produced for sale.[...]

U.S.A.

Danby v. Osteopathic Hospital Ass'n of Delaware
34 Del. Ch. 427, 104 A.2d 903, 1954

TUNNELL, Justice.

[...]

This promise was made to a charitable corporation, and for that reason, we are not confined to the same orthodox concepts which once were applicable to every situation arising within a common law jurisdiction. There can be no denying that the strong desire on the part of the American courts to favor charitable institutions has established a doctrine which once would have been looked upon as legal heresy. Doubtless this judicial attitude is largely responsible for the massive machinery of benevolence to be observed on every side. The reasons announced in justification of these holdings, however, have not always been technically satisfying. Williston on Contracts (Revised Ed.) Vol. I, p.404.

But regardless of its genesis, there can be no doubting the general American rule that while a bare promise to a charity is at first revocable, it does not remain so after the charity, in reliance upon that promise, has put itself into a legal position from which it cannot be expected to extricate itself without substantial injury. This principle is often spoken of as an application of the doctrine of promissory estoppel.[...]

As soon as the contracts were executed, the legal obligation to the contractors presumably bound defendant to complete the job. The 'acceptance' was not the borrowing of the money, but the assumption of the obligation to build the hospital.[...]

This plaintiff, therefore, is within the prohibition of the promissory estoppel rule which applies to charities.[...] There is no real difference between offering to give money to a hospital so that a building can be built and an offer to lend one's credit so that the necessary money can be borrowed and the building built. Both are such offers of assistance as are calculated to induce the hospital to build.

A logical corollary of this rule is that an undertaking to do something which is already obligatory will not furnish the basis of an estoppel.[...]

Chapter Six

Contracts: Good Faith, Estoppel ...

A manifestation of one's will under the form of a juridical act, convention, a contract, an agreement, when it is expressed with the intent to create a binding obligation on the part of one or two or more parties can only be, in last resort, the outward transposition of a 'conscious' intent formulated and expressed by a natural person. Whether in the civil law tradition or the common law tradition, it is the fundamental purpose of the standard contractual legal requirements (only 2 or 3 have been presented above p.39–78, 79–98), when they are all met, to make a contract valid and binding as a result of the parties' intent being channeled through a series of conduits which are identified as capacity, cause/consideration, consent, Beyond these standard contractual requirements, which are relatively easy to identify and describe, there is a concept, a doctrine, or principle or, still, precept of a different nature, and of a much broader scope of application than the law of contracts only. This concept which does not have a purely 'legalistic' meaning and which, for that reason, is difficult, vel non impossible to contain within a definition acceptable by all, is that of "good faith." Should contractual relations, our focus here, be governed by such a principle which we find expressed in Justinian's Institutes under the form of "Justitia" which is described as "the constant and perpetual disposition to render every man his due?" We also find in the Institutes that "the precepts of the law are, to live honestly, to hurt no one, to give every one his due." For our limited purpose, we are going to equate Justinian's "words of wisdom" with the 'civil law' concept of "good faith" in contracts. [The Institutes of Justinian, Title I, D.1. T.1 § 1 and § 3].

If we wish to look for a "common law" source of guidance and inspiration to parallel (if at all possible!) Justinian's precepts for the civil law, we suggest the following: "These are the eternal immutable laws of good and evil ... which are necessary for the conduct of human actions. Such, among others are these principles: that we should live honestly, should hurt nobody, and should render to every one his due; to which three general principles Justinian has reduced the whole doctrine of law." [W. Blackstone, Commentaries on the Laws of England in Four Books, Introduction, Section II Of the Nature of Laws in General, by George Sharswood, 1860]

Does this 'parallel' between Justinian and Blackstone lead to a 'parallel' approach of the civil law and the common law to the concept of 'good faith?' Actually "[T]o the civilian mind, good faith is a broad reaching concept that covers far more territory than the comparable provision of Uniform Commercial Code 1-203, which requires good faith in the performance of contracts. English law, at the opposite extreme from the civilians, adamantly refuses to recognize any such duty of good faith whatsoever. The common lawyers at UNCITRAL, uneasy with the vague and expansive civilian concept of good faith performance, adamantly refused to accept a provision in the Vienna Convention requiring good faith performance; the civilians sternly insisted on the inclusion of such a provision. Which camp prevailed?"(Comparative Law, An Introduction, Vivian Grosswald Curran, Carolina Academic Press, 2002, p.107)

Indeed, the common law and the civil law have, in the field of contract (in civil law) or contracts (in common law), somewhat different approaches to those precepts of the law as Justinian and, centuries later, Blackstone expressed them. At civil law, the concept of "good faith" has played, for centuries, and still play, today, a major role in the *theory* of the law of contract. Most civil law systems, because of their inherent ability at elaborating theories, are referring to this single and comprehensive concept of "good faith" to cover, but not to its full civil law extent, a variety of concepts used by the common law in different contexts. Despite their variety, such concepts have nevertheless a common foundation which is to bring some 'fairness,' 'equity,' 'balance' to contractual transactions. The common law will call upon such concepts as 'consideration,' or 'unconscionability,' or 'estoppel,' or 'reliance' and even 'good faith.' Hence the long title of this Section to reconcile the civil law and the common law on one "common line"!

A: "Good Faith" in the Civil Law

BGB

Section 157 Interpretation of contracts

Contracts are to be interpreted according to the requirements of good faith, taking common usage into consideration

Section 242 Performance in good faith

The obligor must perform in a manner consistent with good faith taking into account common usage.

[See also Sections:122, 123, 311.]

La. Civ. C.

Article 1759: Good faith shall govern the conduct of the obligor and the obligee in whatever pertains to the obligation.

Article 1770 (2): A resolutory condition that depends solely on the will of the obligor must be fulfilled in good faith.

Article 1975: The quantity of a contractual object may be determined by the output of one party or the requirements of the other.

In such a case, output or requirements must be measured in good faith.

Article 1983: Contracts have the effect of law for the parties and may be dissolved only through the consent of the parties or on grounds provided by law. Contracts must be performed in good faith.

Article 2028(2): Counterletters can have no effects against third parties in good faith.

Article 2035(1): Nullity of a contract does not impair the rights acquired through an onerous contract by a third party in good faith.

Fr. Civ. C.

Article 1134: Conventions legally entered into have the effect of law for the parties.

They may be revoked only by their mutual consent or on grounds provided by legislation.

They must be performed in good faith.

Article 1135: Conventions are binding not only as to what they expressly state, but also as to all that equity, usage or statute relate to an obligation according to its nature.

Article 1156: One must in conventions seek what is the common intention of the contracting parties, rather than adhere to the literal meaning of words.

C.C.Q.

Article 1375: The parties shall conduct themselves in good faith both at the time the obligation is created and at the time it is performed or extinguished.

Article 1397: A contract made in violation of a promise to contract may be set up against the beneficiary of the promise, but without affecting his remedy for damages against the promisor and the person having contracted in bad faith with the promisor.

The same rule applies to a contract made in violation of a first refusal agreement.

Article 1426: In interpreting a contract, the nature of the contract, the circumstances in which it was formed, the interpretation which has already been given to it by the parties or which it may have received, and usage, are all taken into account.

Article 1434: A contract validly formed binds the parties who have entered into it not only as to what they have expressed in it but also as to what is incident to it according to its nature and in conformity with usage, equity or law.

Article 1452:Third persons in good faith may, according to their interest, avail themselves of the apparent contract or the counter letter; however, where conflicts of interest arise between them, preference is given to the person who avails himself of the apparent contract.

Sw. Civ. C.

Article 2: Every person is bound to exercise his rights and fulfill his obligations according to the principles of good faith.

The law does not sanction the evident abuse of a person's rights.

Article 3: *Bona fides* is presumed whenever the existence of a right has been expressly made to depend on the observance of good faith.

No person can plead *bona fides* in any case where he has failed to exercise the degree of care required by the circumstances.

It. Civ. C.

Article 1337: Negotiations and pre-contractual liability. "The parties, in the conduct of negotiations and the formation of the contract, shall conduct themselves according to good faith."

Article 1338: Knowledge of reasons for invalidity. "A party who knows or should know the existence of a reason for invalidity of the contract and does not give notice to the other party is bound to compensate for the damage suffered by the latter in relying, without fault, on the validity of the contract."

Article 1366: Interpretation according to good faith. "The contract shall be interpreted according to good faith."

Article 1375: Performance according to good faith. "The contract shall be performed according to good faith."

Article 1391: (Representation) Material subjective conditions. In cases in which it is material to ascertain the existence of good or bad faith or of knowledge or ignorance of certain circumstances, regard is had to the representative, unless the matters at stake were predetermined by the principal.

In no case can a principal who is in bad faith take advantage of the ignorance or good faith of a representative."

Article 1460:(Dissolution of Contract) Defense based upon non-performance. In contracts providing for mutual counterperformance, each party can refuse to perform his obligation if the other party does not perform or offer to perform his own at the same time, unless different times for performance have been established by the parties or appear from the nature of the contract.

However, performance cannot be rejected if, considering the circumstances, such rejection is contrary to good faith."

Planiol et Ripert Vol. VI Obligations LGDJ
1952

§ 379 quater. Good faith. Conventions must be performed in good faith, states Article 1134. Inherited from Roman law wherein, besides the other meanings it still has today, good faith had a precise meaning only in the actions in good faith as opposed to actions based on law in the narrow sense of the word, today the concept of good faith in Article 1134 has only a more ambiguous scope of application. It means that any contracting party must act as an honest person in whatever relates to the performance of the contract. Not to act as an honest person amounts to being at fault.... .In any case, it is useful to resort to an expression to refer to a breach of the duty of honesty which arises from the fact that one has bound himself by a contract.[27]

Malaurie, Aynès et Stoffel-Munck
Les Obligations, Defrénois 2003.

464. Negotiations. [...] Two principles, apparently in conflict with each other, govern the matter. On the one hand, the freedom to terminate the ne-

---

27. Liberal translation by author

gotiations without incurring any liability;.... On the other hand, the obligation of good faith in negotiations, to carry out the negotiation process in a fair and honest manner; hence the following duties: to inform in an honest manner the other party to the contract; to grant him a reasonable time to think about it; to attempt to reach an agreement; not to seek to introduce unacceptable conditions or dilatory measures....

764. **An expanding principle** ... Good faith, in the execution as well as in the formation of a contract, amounts to each party not betraying the confidence created by the willingness to enter into a contract; such an expectation is at the heart of the contract particularly when the contractual relationship is to last over a period of time. It is the embodiment of the general duty of honest and fair behavior, which does exist in many other branches of the law: criminal and civil procedure,..competition ... ; the opposite of fairness and honesty is duplicity ... which undermines the long term expectations ... Good faith is the mere extension of the binding force of a contract, rather than a limitation imposed on the creditor; the latter is not required to waive his right or interest in the name of some vague juridical solidarity but, instead, to give the contract its full force to an extent compatible with his own personal interest ... [28]

Fredrich Kessler and Edith Fine,
Culpa In Contrahendo, Bargaining In Good Faith, And Freedom Of Contract: A Comparative Study
[77 Harv. L. Rev. 401, 1964]

The doctrine of *culpa in contrahendo* goes back to a famous article by Jhering, published in 1861, entitled "*Culpa in contrahendo, oder Schadensersatz bei nichtigen oder nicht zur Perfektion gelangten Verträgen.*" It advanced the thesis that damages should be recoverable against the party whose blameworthy conduct during negotiations for a contract brought about its invalidity or prevented its perfection. Its impact has reached beyond the German law of contracts ... Going beyond a mere correction of the will dogma, *culpa in contrahendo* became anchored in the great principle of good faith and fair dealing which permeates, we are told, the whole law of contracts, controlling, indeed, all legal transactions ... Once parties enter into negotiations for a contract, the sweeping language of the cases informs us, a relationship of trust and confidence comes into existence, irrespective of whether they suc-

---

28. Liberal translation by the author.

ceed or fail. Thus, protection is accorded against blameworthy conduct which prevents the consummation of a contract.... Of particular importance are the duties of disclosure imposed on negotiating parties in the interest of fair dealing and the security of transactions. Each party is bound to disclose such matters as are clearly of importance for the other party's decision, provided the latter is unable to procure the information himself and the nondisclosing party is aware of the fact.... [T]he classification of *culpa in contrahendo* liability as contractual, which is constantly emphasized, is of great practical importance due to the inadequacy of tort law ... The impact of Jhering's thesis has not been confined to the German law of contracts. *Culpa in contrahendo* doctrine has profoundly affected Austrian and Swiss law ... To sum up: whatever their theoretical basis or range of application, notions of good faith in the form of *culpa in contrahendo* or otherwise have become firmly established in the civil law system ...

B: "Good Faith" in the Common Law: Consideration, Estoppel, Reliance, Good Faith ...

1. Law of the United Kingdom

P.S. Atiyah

(opus cited)

THE FAIR EXCHANGE (p.167–169)

We should begin by noting that in the latter half of the eighteenth century there were signs of an emerging principle of good faith in contract law. The idea of good faith would, of course, have been completely congruent with traditional morality, though it needed someone like Mansfield to enunciate and apply the principle in a wide variety of cases. Mansfield began this task, but it was never completed, for the economic liberalism which he also favoured and helped to develop, ultimately proved fatal to anything as paternalistic as a general principle of good faith.[...] in *Carter* v. *Boehm* Lord Mansfield placed this decision on the broad principle of good faith, and made it quite clear that he envisaged this principle as one applicable to all transactions. 'The governing principle,' he said, 'is applicable to all contracts and dealings. Good faith forbids either party, by concealing what he privately knows, to draw the other into a bargain, from his ignorance of that fact and his believing the contrary. […] In *Bexwell* v. *Christie* Mansfield held that a person who put up something for sale by auction and advertised that it would be sold to the highest bidder committed a gross fraud if he surreptitiously employed someone to bid himself.[…] the next case along these lines came before the Common Pleas in 1825 when Best C.J. was presiding; and Best C.J. was an old-fashioned judge with a strong moral sense somewhat in the eighteenth-century tradition. He agreed entirely with Mansfield's judgment and carried his Court with him. The result was that this rule survived the new nineteenth-century doctrines, and is still with us.

Butterworths

(opus cited)

1.80 Whilst English contract lawyers have long been familiar with the concept of (subjective) good faith in the sense of honesty in fact or a clear conscience—an idea to be found, for instance, in the context of negotiable instruments and the sale of property—until quite recently, the idea of a general doctrine of good faith, in the sense of an overriding (and objective) requirement of fair dealing, was not part of the lexicon of English contract law. Or, at any rate, it was not part of the lexicon in the twentieth century. With the exception of Raphael Powell's inaugural lecture in 1956, good faith in contract was not a topic addressed by academics or textbook writers; nor was a violation of the principle of good faith a matter openly pleaded or addressed in litigation, although references to bad faith occasionally appeared explicitly or implicitly in judicial opinions.

1.87 […], the case against the adoption of a general principle of good faith is that English contract law is premised on adversarial self-interested dealing (rather than other-regarding good faith dealing); that good faith is a vague idea, threatening to import an uncertain discretion into English law; that the implementation of a good faith doctrine would call for difficult inquiries into contracting parties' reasons in particular cases; that good faith represents a challenge to the autonomy of contracting parties; and, that a general doctrine cannot be appropriate when contracting contexts vary so much—in particular, harking back to the first objection, a general doctrine of good faith would make little sense in those contracting contexts in which the participants regulate their dealings in a way that openly tolerates opportunism.

1.89 The paradigm of neutrality holds: (i) that there is a strict equivalence between a general doctrine of good faith and the piecemeal provisions of

English law that regulate fair dealing (we can call this 'the equivalence the-sis'); and (ii) that it makes no difference whether English law operates with a general doctrine of with piecemeal provisions (we can call this 'the indiffer-ence thesis').

Good faith and reasonableness

1.103 There is an obvious symmetry in debates about the adoption of gen-eral principles of good faith and/or reasonableness. Those who advocate that English law (or, indeed, any modern common law system) should adopt such general principles must overcome two fundamental objections: first, that there is no reason why contracting should be subjected to moral con-straints — it is simply a matter of parties pursuing their own self-interest; and, secondly, that if moral constraints are to be introduced, this unwork-able until agreement is reached about whose (or which) morality is to serve as the reference point for such doctrines. [....] what we might anticipate in the modern law of contract in England, in which the notion of reasonable-ness (if not that of good faith) abounds, is a tendency for doctrine to reflect the expectations associated with good practice [...] In other words, we might expect that English law will move towards the adoption of good faith as a requirement (in substance, if not in name) ...

2. United States Law

Restatement, 2d

§ 205. Duty of Good Faith and Fair Dealing

Every contract imposes upon each party a duty of good faith and fair dealing in its performance and its enforcement.

Comment: *a. Meaning of "good faith."* ... The phrase "good faith" is used in a variety of contexts, and its meaning varies somewhat with the context. Good faith performance or enforcement of a contract emphasizes faithful-ness to an agreed common purpose and consistency with the justified expec-tations of the other party; it excludes a variety of types of conduct character-ized as involving "bad faith" because they violate community standards of decency, fairness or reasonableness ...

c. Good faith in negotiation. This Section ... does not deal with good faith in the formation of a contract. Bad faith in negotiation, although not within the scope of this Section, may be subject to sanctions. Particular forms of bad faith in bargaining are the subjects of rules as to capacity to contract, mutual assent and consideration and of rules as to invalidating causes such as fraud and duress.

d. Good faith performance. Subterfuges and evasions violate the obligation of good faith in performance even though the actor believes his conduct to be justified. But the obligation goes further: bad faith may be overt or may consist of inaction, and fair dealing may require more than honesty. …

[See also Restatement 2d: § 157 (Mistakes) — § 161 (Misrepresentation) — § 172 (id) — § 176 (Duress and Undue Influence]

UCC

§ 1-201. General Definitions.

(20) "Good faith," except as otherwise provided in Article 5, means honesty in fact and the observance of reasonable commercial standards of fair dealing.

§ 1-302. Variation by Agreement.

(b) The obligations of good faith, diligence reasonableness, and care prescribed by [the Uniform Commercial Code] may not be disclaimed by agreement. The parties, by agreement, may determine the standards by which the performance of those obligations is to be measured if those standards are not manifestly unreasonable. Whenever [the Uniform Commercial Code] requires an action to be taken within a reasonable time, a time that is not manifestly unreasonable may be fixed by agreement.

§ 1-304. Obligation of Good Faith.

Every contract or duty within [the Uniform Commercial Code] imposes an obligation of good faith in its performance and enforcement.

Official Comment

1. This section sets forth a basic principle running throughout the Uniform Commercial Code.… This section means that a failure to perform or enforce, in good faith, a specific duty or obligation under the contract, constitutes a breach of that contract or makes unavailable, under the particular circumstances, a remedial right or power …

[See also, for example: ARTICLE 2 **Sales; §2-103** (j); **§2-302. Uncon-scionable Contract or Term; §2-305. Open Price Term; §2-306. Output, Re-quirements and Exclusive Dealings;** etc ...]

John D. Calamari and Joseph M. Perillo
The Law of Contracts, 4th ed.
West 1998

§11.38 Good Faith

(a) Introduction

Despite a promising beginning in the eighteenth century, "the common law has traditionally been reluctant to recognize, at least as overt doctrine, any generalized duty to act in good faith toward others in social intercourse"(Holmes). This approach was solidified with the development, "during the nineteenth century, of the pure theory of contract characterized by notions of volition, *laissez-faire,* freedom of contract, judicial noninter-vention and bargained-for-exchange." (Holmes) In the twentieth century doctrines of promissory estoppel, unconscionability and modern theories of quasi-contract have changed these rigid notions. As part of the same devel-opment, "modern contract law appears to support and promote good faith conduct based on reasonable standards in the formation, performance and discharge of contracts."(Holmes).The UCC and Second Restatement have been influential in bringing about this result.

(b) Relationship to Other Portions of Text

[...] The concept of good faith is used in the chapter on consideration with respect to the termination of an agreement, illusory promises, the sur-render of an invalid claim and output and requirements contracts. The con-cept is also used in the area of duress. In promissory estoppel doctrine, the notion of culpa in contrahendo is based on a duty to bargain in good faith.... Although there is an obligation of good faith implicit in all con-tracts, there is nothing to prevent the parties from having an explicit provi-sion elaborating the scope of the duty.

E. Allan Farnsworth
(opus cited)

§3.26. Precontractual Liability. Courts have traditionally accorded parties the freedom to negotiate without risk of precontractual liability. If the negotiations *succeed* and result in ultimate agreement, a party that has behaved improperly can be deprived of the bargain on the ground of misrepresentation, duress, undue influence, or unconscionability. But if the negotiations *fail* because of similar behavior, courts have been reluctant to impose precontractual liability. Although a duty of fair dealing is now generally imposed on the parties to an existing contract, that duty is not so formulated as to extend to negotiations before the contract is made. Under an existing contract each party, though free to refuse to negotiate a modification, is bound, once negotiations have begun, by a duty of good faith and fair dealing imposed by that contract. In sharp contrast, courts traditionally take a view of the precontractual period that assures a broad freedom of negotiation and relieves a party of the risk of liability arising during negotiation. As a general rule, a party to precontractual negotiations may break them off without liability at any time and for any reason—a change of heart, a change of circumstances, a better deal—or for no reason at all. The only cost of doing so is the loss of that party's own investment in the negotiations in terms of time, effort, and expense.[....] In recent decades, courts have shown increasing willingness to impose precontractual liability. The possible grounds can be grouped under four headings: (1)unjust enrichment resulting from the negotiations; (2) a misrepresentation made during the negotiations; (3) a specific promise made during the negotiations; (4) an agreement to negotiate in good faith.

POSNER, Circuit Judge, 7th Circuit, United States Court of Appeals.

"[...] [W]e must consider the meaning of the contract duty of "good faith" ... We do so mindful of Learned Hand's warning, that "such words as 'fraud,' 'good faith,' 'whim.'... obscure the issue" ... The duty of honesty, of good faith even expansively conceived, is not a duty of candor ... Before the contract is signed, the parties confront each other with a natural wariness. Neither expects the other to be particularly forthcoming, and therefore there is no deception when one is not. Afterwards the situation is different. The parties are now in a cooperative relationship the costs of which will be considerably reduced by a measure of trust. So each lowers his guard a bit, and now silence is more apt to be deceptive ... The concept of duty of good faith like the concept of fiduciary duty is a stab at approximating the terms the parties would have negotiated had they foreseen the circumstances that have given rise to their dispute. The parties want to minimize the costs of performance. To the extent that a doctrine of good faith designed to do this by reducing defensive expenditures is a reasonable measure to this end, interpolating it into the contract advances the parties' joint goal ... The office of the doctrine of good faith is to forbid the kinds of opportunistic behavior that a mutually dependent, cooperative relationship might enable in the absence of rule. "Good faith" is a compact reference to an implied undertaking not to take opportunistic advantage in a way that could have been contemplated at the time of drafting, and which therefore was not resolved explicitly by the parties" ... The contractual duty of good faith is thus not some newfangled bit of welfare-state paternalism or the sediment of an altruistic strain in contract law, and we are therefore not surprised to find the essentials of the modern doctrine well established in nineteenth-century cases ... The formation or negotiation state is precontractual, and here the duty is minimized. It is greater not only at the performance but also at the enforcement stage, which is also postcontractual ... At the formation of the contract the parties are dealing in present realities; performance still lies in the future. As performance unfolds, circumstances change, often unforeseeably; the explicit terms of the contract become progressively less apt to the governance of the parties' relationship; and the role of implied conditions—and with it the scope and bite of the good-faith doctrine—grows ... [W]hether we say that a contract shall be deemed to contain such implied conditions as are necessary to make sense of the contract, or that a contract obligates the parties to cooperate in its performance in "good faith" to the extent necessary to carry out the purposes of the contract, comes to much the same thing. They are different ways of formulating the overriding purpose of contract law, which is to give the parties what they would have stipulated for expressly if at the time of making the contract they had had complete knowledge of the future and the costs of negotiating and adding provisions to the contract had been zero...." [Market Street Associates Limited Partnership v. Dale Frey, et al., 941 F.2d 588, 1991]

C: "Good Faith" in International/Multinational Law

CISG

Article 7. (1) In the interpretation of this Convention, regard is to be had to its international character and to the need to promote uniformity in its application and the observance of good faith in international trade.

Article 9. (2) The parties are considered, unless otherwise agreed, to have impliedly made applicable to their contract or its formation a usage of which the parties knew or ought to have known and which in international trade is widely known to, and regularly observed by, parties to contracts of the type involved in the particular trade concerned.

[See also, CISG Articles 77, 79 and 80]

UNIDROIT

Article 1.7: (1) Each party must act in accordance with good faith and fair dealing in international trade. (2)..

Article 2.1.15: (1) A party is free to negotiate and is not liable for failure to reach an agreement. (2) However, a party who negotiates or breaks off negotiations in bad faith is liable for the losses caused to the other party. (3) It is bad faith, in particular, for a party to enter into or continue negotiations when intending not to reach an agreement with the other party.

Article 4.8: (1) Where the parties to a contract have not agreed with respect to a term which is important for a determination of their rights and duties, a term which is appropriate in the circumstances shall be supplied.(2) In determining what is an appropriate term regard shall be had, among other factors, to (a) the intention of the parties; (b) the nature and purpose of the contract; (c) good faith and fair dealing;(d) reasonableness.

Article 5.1.2: Implied obligations stem from (a) the nature and purpose of the contract; (b) practices established between the parties and usages; (c) good faith and fair dealing; (d) reasonableness.

[See also, UNIDROIT: Articles 3.10 (Gross Disparity); 7.1.6 (Exemption clauses); 7.1.7 (Force Majeure).

Principles of European Contract Law

Article 1:102: Freedom of Contract

(1) Parties are free to enter into a contract and to determine its contents, subject to the requirements of good faith and fair dealing, and the mandatory rules established by these Principles. (2) The parties may exclude the application of any of these Principles or derogate from or vary their effects, except as otherwise provided by theses Principles.

Article 1:106: Interpretation and Supplementation

(1) These Principles should be interpreted and developed in accordance with their purposes. In particular, regard should be had to the need to promote good faith and fair dealing, certainly in contractual relationships and uniformity of application.(2) ...

Article 1:201: Good Faith and Fair Dealing

(1) Each party must act in accordance with good faith and fair dealing. (2) The parties may not exclude or limit this duty.

Article 1: 202: Duty to Co-operate

Each party owes to the other a duty to co-operate in order to give full effect to the contract.

Article 2: 301: Negotiations Contrary to Good Faith

(1) A party is free to negotiate and is not liable for failure to reach an agreement.

(2) However, a party which has negotiated or broken off negotiations contrary to good faith and fair dealing is liable for the losses caused to the other party.

(3) It is contrary to good faith and fair dealing, in particular, for a party to enter into or continue negotiations with no real intention of reaching an agreement with the other party.

Article 5:102: Relevant Circumstances (Interpretation)

In interpreting the contract, regard shall be had, in particular, to:

(a) to (f): (g) good faith and fair dealing.

[See also, PECL: Articles 4:107 (Fraud); 6:102 (Implied Terms); 8: 109 (Clause Excluding or Restricting Remedies)

COUNCIL DIRECTIVE 93/13/EEC of 5 April 1993 on unfair terms in consumer contracts

Article 3. 1. A contractual term which has not been individually negotiated shall be regarded as unfair if, contrary to the requirement of good faith, it causes a significant imbalance in the parties' rights and obligations arising under the contract, to the detriment of the consumer.

DIRECTIVE 2005/29/EC OF THE EUROPEAN PARLIAMENT AND OF THE COUNCIL OF 11 May 2005 (Unfair Commercial Practices Directive)

Article 2 Definitions: (j) "undue influence" means exploiting a position of power in relation to the consumer so as to apply pressure, even without using or threatening to use physical force, in a way which significantly limits the consumer's ability to make an informed decision;

Article 3 Scope: 1. This Directive shall apply to unfair business-to-consumer commercial practices … before, during and after a commercial transaction in relation to a product.

D. Courts' Decisions

1. Civil Law Cases

France

Société Alain Manoukian c. Consorts Wajsfisz
Com., 23 nov.2003, Bull. civ. IV no 186 p.206, 2003

[Facts: summary: Alain Manoukian Inc, entered into negotiations with the spouses Wajfisz, shareholders of Stuck Inc.; the purpose of the negotiations was the transfer of the shares making up the capital of Stuck Inc. After meetings, exchange of correspondence during the spring 1997, the negotiations led, in Sept.1997, to a tentative agreement that included a series of suspensive conditions to be met before Oct. 10 postponed to the 31st. Subsequent to new requests for modifications, Manoukian agreed to postpone until Nov.15, 1997 the actual occurrence of the suspensive conditions. On Nov. 13, 1997, the Wajsfisz were provided with a new draft for the transfer of the shares; on Nov.24, Manoukian Inc. learned that the Wajsfisz had entered into a promise to transfer the shares to Les Complices Inc.; Manoukian brought an action against the Wajsfisz and Les Complices for wrongful (bad faith) breach of the negotiations.]

[The Court]: … The Court of Appeal held that the spouses Wajsfisz had unilaterally and in bad faith broken the negotiations that they never appeared to intend to abandon whereas Manoukian Inc. continued to negotiate normally; on the basis of these observations and assessments, the Court of Appeal provided the proper legal foundation for its decision;

… However, considering that the circumstances constitutive of a fault committed in the exercise of the right to unilaterally breakup pre-contractual negotiations are not the cause of the prejudice amounting to the loss of the chance to make a profit which the perfection of the contract would allow one to hope for … [The Chambre Commerciale ruled that Manoukian could receive back the expenses incurred because of the negotiations and the research conducted, but that Manoukian could not get the 'profit' they were hoping to make … had the contract been perfected]

Québec
National Bank of Canada c. Dame Soucisse and others
[1981] 2 R.C.S. 339

BEETZ J.

[Facts omitted]

[...] I would not hesitate to hold that, to the extent that it wished to make new advances after the surety's death on the basis of the letters of suretyship, the *Bank* was under an obligation as soon as it learned of the death itself to disclose to the heirs of the surety that these suretyships existed and were revocable. [...] I would hold that this obligation results from the principle that agreements must be performed in good faith. It is true that no provision is to be found in our *Civil Code* which states this expressly, like art. 1134 of the *Code Napoléon*, but Mignault (*op cit.,* Vol. 5, at pp.261 and 264) properly observes that the principle is axiomatic and that agreements must be performed in good faith because [translation] "we no longer have, as in Roman law, contracts *bonae fidei* and contracts *stricti juris*".[...]

Because the *Bank* was at fault in not disclosing the existence of the letters of suretyship to the heirs of the surety and, so preventing them from revoking, the *Bank* is in my opinion not in a position to argue that it made new advances to the debtors in reliance on these letters. Its action against the heirs of the surety is also inadmissible because no one should profit from his own fault or seek the aid of the courts in doing so. [...]

Germany
BGHZ 69, 53, VIII. Civil Senate
(VIII ZR 186/75) (engl. translation) in the web site of the University of Texas School of Law[29]

In 1961, B., a civil engineering company experienced increasing financial difficulties. In order to save the firm from bankruptcy and to restore it to financial soundness, the defendant became involved in it financially and managerially. By transforming the one-man company B. into a GmbH & Co. KG (limited liability company)(hereafter called: the KG), he acquired 51% of

---

29. http://www.utexas.edu/law/academics/centers/transnational/work/,[copyright holder].

the shares in the limited company in June 1962 and 51% in the unlimited partnership forming part of the company.

From August 1962 the defendant tried to sell his shares in the KG. He offered these to the claimant and presented him, during sales discussion, with the KG's "consolidated accounts for 31 August 1962" which showed a profit of DM 10, 444. As a result, the claimant , by contracts of 21 February 1963, acquired from the defendant various shares totalling DM 1,090,500.

By this action, the claimant demands from the defendant damages amounting to a partial instalment of DM 1,750,000. As a reason for the claim the claimant stated that the defendant, by forging the true financial situation as of 31 August 1962, had in bad faith pretended that the KG had already made a profit, though a small one, and was thus out of the red, although in reality the company at that time was suffering considerable and continuously growing losses with the result that the claimant could only save the company by "financial injections" amounting to nearly DM 8 million and by taking over or paying sureties of more than DM 3 million. As late as directly before conclusion of the contract, the defendant, according to his own admission, had on request guaranteed that the company's financial status as shown per 31 August 1962 was unchanged. With full knowledge of the company's actual financial and profit situation, the claimant would not have agreed to participate in the company.

The defendant denies having deceived the claimant. The KG's financial improvement, apparent since August 1962, could soon have resulted in the company's profitability if the claimant had made sensible and sufficient capital investments. In addition, the claimant, who through the KG had later on gained orders in excess of DM 200 million, had from the start only intended to gain a foothold in the Southern German market through its shares in the KG.

The Landgericht has rejected the claim, the appeal court has ordered the defendant to pay DM 705, 018. 32. The further appeal of both parties results in a partial quashing of the appeal court's judgment and a referral back to that court for further investigations.

Reasons

I.

1. The appeal court held that there is insufficient evidence for the claimant having intentionally been deceived by the defendant, but it acknowledged in principle the claim for damages for reasons of culpa in contrahendo. The KG's consolidated financial statement as of 31 August 1962, on which the

claimant first and foremost based his decision to acquire the shares, had been drawn up incorrectly and in contravention of the rules on proper balance sheet procedures by employees of the defendant for whose conduct the latter is liable. [...]

2. These findings of the appeal court withstand the defendant's arguments raised in his further appeal, at least as there result is concerned ... (further deliberations).

II.

1.

2. It appears that these findings are influenced by a legal error.

a) The appeal court correctly presumes that a person who has experienced losses from culpa in contrahendo can claim compensation for his damage caused by breach of trust, which itself is however not limited by his interests in the performance of the contract but can, in specific cases, then exceed those interests [...]. The party experiencing damage can thus demand to be put into the same position as he would be in had the illegal action not taken place [...]. In view of the multiple forms which culpa in contrahendo can take, exactly what kind of damage is capable of compensation depends, [...] on the causal link between the damaging conduct and the specific damage which occurred in each particular case [...].

b) The current case belongs to the typical cases in which a contract would not have been entered into without the damaging conduct, i.e. the incorrect statement as to the losses at the time when the contract was signed. As part of this assessment of the facts, the appeal court comes to the legally correct conclusion that the claimant would not have decided to buy the shares from the defendant if he had known that, at the time of signing the contract, the balance sheets showed a loss of DM 1, 522, 204.53. [...] Under these conditions and by mutual reversed transactions in respect of the contract, damages are in principle to be calculated according to the expenditures needlessly made by the damaged party while trusting in the correctness of the information given by the damaging party [...].

c) But the case here under consideration is special insofar as the buyer wishes now to stick firmly to the contract which he would not have entered into if he had initially known the true circumstances. He does this either because he thinks such course of action to be sound economically or because at the time, when he became aware of the seller's untrue statements, he had already integrated the acquired enterprise so deeply into his own group of enterprises that reversing the transaction could only be achieved with very great difficulties. In such a case, the above-mentioned method of calculating the damage can not lead to a just determination of the damage to be compensated for if only because a retransfer of both parties' performances does not come into play. And as the appeal court rightly states, under these circumstances, the claimant would have to agree to an offsetting of his expenditures incurred in the form of the so-called "financial injections" against his unquestionably much higher profits gained from the KG. Under this method of calculation no damage would be compensated, although the claimant, looking at the deal objectively and with hindsight, has spent more capital for the acquisition of the KG's share than he would have had to find if he had known fully the true financial situation. Finally, the appeal court, based on the statements made by the witness Dr. Sch. correctly holds that the claimant had already planned to invest more capital into the KG in order to avert further losses, with the result that no safe delineation can be made between such investment and the "financial injections" which, according to the claimant's submission, had become necessary due to the KG's high losses unknown to him when he concluded the contract

d) If one aims at all sensibly to ascertain the damage incurred, where the buyer wishes to stick to the contract, he must be treated as if he had succeeded in full knowledge of the true facts in concluding the contract for a much more favourable price [...] there is then no need for any hypothetical proof, which can anyhow hardly be obtained, that the seller himself would have agreed to conclude a contract given these new conditions. Here, damage is the amount which the claimant overspent when buying the defendant's share in the KG, because his trust in the truth of the financial statements made had been abused.

e) ...

2. Common Law Cases

U.K.

Interfoto Picture Library Ltd. v.
Stiletto Visual Programmes Ltd.
[1989] 1 Q.B. 433

[Facts: The plaintiffs ran a photographic transparency lending library. Following a telephone inquiry by the defendants, the plaintiffs delivered to them 47 transparencies together with a delivery note containing nine printed conditions. Condition 2 stipulated that all the transparencies had to be returned within 14 days of delivery otherwise a holding fee of £5 a day and value added tax would be charged for each transparency retained thereafter. The defendants, who had not used the plaintiffs' services before, did not read the conditions and returned the transparencies four weeks later whereupon the plaintiffs invoiced the defendants for £3, 783.50. The defendants refused to pay and the plaintiffs brought an action to recover that sum.]

DILLIN L.J.

[...]

There was never any oral discussion of terms between the parties before the contract was made. In particular there was no discussion whatever of terms in the original telephone conversation when Mr. Beeching made his preliminary inquiry. The question is therefore whether condition 2 was sufficiently brought to the defendants' attention to make it a term of the contract which was only concluded after the defendants had received, and must have known that they had received the transparencies *and* the delivery note. [...]

More recently the question has been discussed whether it is enough to look at a set of printed conditions as a whole. When for instance one condition in a set is particularly onerous does something special need to be done to draw customers' attention to that particular condition?[...]

Condition 2 of these plaintiffs' conditions is in my judgment a very onerous clause. The defendants could not conceivably have known, if their attention was not drawn to the clause, that the plaintiffs were proposing to charge a "holding fee" for the retention of the transparencies at such a very high and exorbitant rate.[...]

In the present case, nothing whatever was done by the plaintiffs to draw the defendants' attention particularly to condition 2; it was merely one of four columns' width of conditions printed across the foot of the delivery note. Consequently condition 2 never, in my judgment, became part of the contract between the parties.[...]

BINGHAM L.J.

In many civil law systems, and perhaps in most legal systems outside the common law world, the law of obligations recognizes and enforces an overriding principle that in making and carrying out contracts parties should act in good faith. This does not simply mean that they should not deceive each other, a principle which any legal system must recognize; its effect is perhaps most aptly conveyed by such metaphorical colloquialisms as "playing fair," "coming clean" or "putting one's cards face upwards on the table." It is in essence a principle of fair and open dealing. In such a forum it might, I think, be held on the facts of this case that the plaintiffs were under a duty in all fairness to draw the defendants' attention specifically to the high price payable if the transparencies were not returned in time and, when the 14 days had expired, to point out to the defendants the high cost of continued failure to return them.

English law has, characteristically, committed itself to no such overriding principle but has developed piecemeal solutions in response to demonstrated problems of unfairness. Many examples could be given. Thus equity has intervened to strike down unconscionable bargains. Parliament has stepped in to regulate the imposition of exemption clauses and the form of certain hire-purchase agreements. The common law also has made its contribution, by holding that certain classes of contract require the utmost good faith, by treating as irrecoverable what purport to be agreed estimates of damage but are in truth a disguised penalty for breach, and in many other ways.

U.S.A.

Market Street Associates Limited Partnership v. Dale Frey, et. al.

941 F .2d 588, 1991

POSNER, Circuit Judge.

Market Street associates Limited Partnership and its general partner appeal from a judgment for the defendants, General Electric Pension Trust and its trustees, entered upon cross-motions for summary judgment in a diversity suit that pivots on the doctrine of "good faith" performance of a contract. […] Wisconsin law applies — common law rather than Uniform Commercial Code, because the contract is for land rather than for goods, and because it is a lease rather than a sale and Wisconsin has not adopted UCC art. 2A, which governs leases.[…]

In 1968, J.C. Penney Company, the retail chain, entered into a sale and lease-back arrangement with General Electric Pension Trust in order to finance Penney's growth. Under the arrangement Penney sold properties to the pension trust which the trust then leased back to Penney for a term of 25 years. Paragraph 34 of the lease entitles the lessee to "request Lessor [the pension trust] to finance the costs and expenses of construction of additional Improvements upon the Premises," [...] Upon receiving the request, the pension trust "agrees to give reasonable consideration to providing the financing of such additional Improvements and Lessor and Lessee shall negotiate in good faith concerning the construction of such Improvements and the financing by Lessor of such costs and expenses."[...]

One of these leases was for a shopping center in Milwaukee. In 1987 Penney assigned this lease to Market Street Associates[...]It decided [...] to try to buy the property back from the pension trust. Market Street Associates' general partner, Orenstein, tried to call David Erb of the pension trust, [...]. Erb did not return his calls, so Orenstein wrote him[...]At first, Erb did not reply. [...] A few days later an associate of Erb called Orenstein and indicated an interest in selling the property for $3 million, which Orenstein considered much too high.

That was in June of 1988. On July 28, Market Street Associates wrote a letter to the pension trust formally requesting funding for $2 million in improvements to the shopping center. The letter made no reference to paragraph 34 of the lease; indeed, it did not mention the lease. The letter asked Erb to call Orenstein to discuss the matter. Erb, in what was becoming a habit of unresponsiveness, did not call. On August 16, Orenstein sent a second letter— certified mail, return receipt requested—again requesting financing and this time referring to the lease, though not expressly to paragraph 34. [...]The very next day, Market Street Associates received from Erb a letter, dated August 10, turning down the original request for financing on the ground that it did not "meet our current investment criteria": [...] On August 22, Orenstein replied to Erb by letter,[...] stating that Market Street Associates would seek financing elsewhere. That was the last contact between the parties until September 27, when Orenstein sent Erb a letter stating that Market Street Associates was exercising the option granted it by paragraph 34 to purchase the property upon the terms specified in that paragraph in the event that negotiations over financing broke down.

The pension trust refused to sell, and this suit to compel specific performance followed. Apparently the price computed by the formula in paragraph 34 is only $1 million. The market value must be higher,[...][30]

The dispositive question in the present case is simply whether Market Street Associates tried to trick the pension trust and succeeded in doing so. If it did, this would be the type of opportunistic behavior in an ongoing contractual

---

30. see supra: Cause and Consideration p.79–98.

relationship that would violate the duty of good faith performance however the duty is formulated.[...]

The facts must be construed as favorably to the nonmoving party, to Market Street Associates, as the record permits [...] When that is done, a different picture emerges. On Market Street Associates' construal of the record, $3 million was a grossly excessive price for the property, and while $1 million might be a bargain it would not confer so great a windfall as to warrant an inference that if the pension trust had known about paragraph 34 it never would have turned down Market Street Associates' request for financing cold. [...] Market Street Associates did not desire financing from the pension trust initially — that is undeniable — yet when it discovered that it could not get financing elsewhere unless it had the title to the property it may have realized that it would have to negotiate with the pension trust over financing before it could hope to buy the property at the price specified in the lease.

On this interpretation of the facts there was no bad faith on the part of Market Street Associates. It acted honestly, reasonably, without ulterior motive, in the face of circumstances as they actually and reasonably appeared to it. The fault was the pension trust's incredible inattention, which misled Market Street Associates into believing that the pension trust had no interest in financing the improvements regardless of the purchase option. We do not usually excuse contracting parties from failing to read and understand the contents of their contract; and in the end what this case comes down to [...] is that an immensely sophisticated enterprise simply failed to read the contract. On the other hand, such enterprises make mistakes just like the rest of us, and deliberately to take advantage of your contracting partner's mistake during the performance stage (for we are not talking about taking advantage of superior knowledge at the formation stage) is a breach of good faith. To be able to correct your contract partner's mistake at zero cost to yourself, and decide not to do so, is a species of opportunistic behavior that the parties would have expressly forbidden in the contract had they foreseen it.[...]

The judgment is reversed ...

Part II
Effects of Contracts

Chapter Seven

Performance-Damages

A: A Comparative Law Perspective

Whenever a party enters into a contractual relationship it is with the expectation to receive "something" in exchange for her own performance. As one knows, there may not, or will not, always be an absolute identity between the performance expected, contemplated in the contract as negotiated and the performance actually received when due. Here again, the civil law and the common law diverge in their approach of the remedies available to the parties and, consequently, in the foundation or justification of these respective remedies. In essence, the divergence between the two legal systems finds its explanation in the "interpretation" one is willing to give of the "intent" of the parties: do they want the very performance they contracted for and, thus, can they have a court enforce the contract by way of specific performance? Or should a "substitute" performance, usually under the form of damages, be sufficient so as to serve as the "equivalent" of the performance expected from the contract?

"[...],[C]ourts in civilian legal systems, routinely grant specific performance by ordering parties to perform their contracts. But courts in common law systems, for reasons that are largely historical, regard specific performance as an "extraordinary "remedy, to be granted only when an award of damages would not be "adequate". (I might add here that we Americans sometimes rationalize the denial of specific performance on the ground that this permits a party to a contract to commit an 'efficient breach,' but that concept of law and economics is one that not only does not travel well, but that struck most of my civilian colleagues as bordering on the immoral.) [E. Allan Farnsworth, A common lawyer's view of his civilian colleagues, 57 La. L. Rev. 227, at 235.]

"[...] The consequences of a binding promise at common law are not affected by the degree of power which the promisor possesses over the promised event. If the promised event does not come to pass, the plaintiff's property is sold to satisfy the damages, with certain limits, which the promisee has suffered by the failure. The consequences are the same in kind whether the promise is that it shall rain, or that another man shall paint a picture, or that the promisor will deliver a bale of cotton. If the legal consequence is the same in all cases, it seems proper that all contracts should be considered from the same legal point of view.... If it be proper to state the common law meaning of promise and contract in this way, it has the advantage of freeing the subject from the superfluous theory that contract is a qualified subjection of one will to another, a kind of limited slavery. It might so regarded if the law compelled men to perform their contracts, of if it allowed promisees to exercise such compulsion ... It is true that in some instances equity does what is called compelling specific performance. But, in the first place, I am speaking of the common law, and, in the next, this only means that equity compels the performance of certain elements of the total promise which are still capable of performance ... The only universal consequence of a legally binding promise is, that the law makes the promisor pay damages if the promised event does not come to pass. In every case it leaves him free from interference until the time for fulfillment has gone by, and therefore free to break his contract if he chooses ... It is true that, when people make contracts, they usually contemplate the performance rather than the breach.... As the relation of contractor and contractee is voluntary, the consequences attaching to the relation must be voluntary. What the event contemplated by the promise is, or in other words what will amount to a breach of contract, is a matter of interpretation and construction. What consequences of the breach are assumed is more remotely, in like manner, a matter of construction, having regard to the circumstances under which the contract is made ..." [O.W. Holmes, Jr. , The Common Law, 1881 at 299 et seq.]

"[In an American law school ...]. We are trained to find ways of getting around or out of contracts, and, as lawyers, we occasionally even counsel clients to breach them. Civil lawyers, on the other hand, are much more committed to elaborating a legal mechanism to enforce as precisely as possible those promises that are actually made and intended..This part of their law is more systematized and coherent than is ours. These differences suggest that more is at stake than simply deciding where a particular loss should fall.

Civilians justify their system by reference to the maxim *pacta sunt servanda*. This "basic and it seems universally accepted principle of contract law" means, in the civil law, that promises are binding ... As René David has explained, "the principle satisfies our philosophical and moral views; it is proper for individuals to be bound by their promises." ... To the civilian mind, the maxim is entirely self-evident ... René David believed the proper translation to be this: "commitments that have been made must be performed." ... American courts, however, generally adopt a translation that applies the maxim only to agreements: "agreements must be obeyed" ... ; "agreements must be respected" ... ; "agreements must be observed" ... The dispute about whether to apply the *pacta* maxim to all promises or only to those that produce agreements is only one of the interesting translation question. Another is how to express the obligation ... The *pacta* maxim is not found in the *Digest*. What most closely resembles it is Ulpian's report of the praetor's rule ... quoted in the chapter *De pactis*: ... (The praetor says: " I will enforce agreements in the form of a pact which have been made neither maliciously nor in contravention of a statute, plebiscite, decree of the senate or edict of the emperor, nor as a fraud on any of these").(Digest 2.14.7.7.).... What is important here is that the *pacta* maxim is not Roman. Whatever the Roman jurists believed about the enforceability of agreements, they did not phrase their belief in terms of *pacta sunt servanda*.... The pacta maxim, slightly altered, appears as an unofficial heading to the first chapter of the *De pactis* title of the *Decretals* of Gregory IX (Pacts, however naked, must be kept) ... What is doubtlessly correct is that the canonists were instrumental in the evolution from formalism to consensualism and therefore contributed substantially to the modern law of contract. What is less certain is how the *pacta* maxim is connected to this process ..." [Richard Hyland, *Pacta Sunt Servanda*: A Meditation, 34 Va. J. Int. L. 405 et seq.]

"[...] The binding nature of a promise is of utmost importance to the civil law, and the courts accordingly bind individuals to their promises ... As Professors Flour and Aubert write ...'morality dominates civilian contract law. They state unequivocally that "the legal obligation incumbent on the contracting party to perform is none other than the moral duty to honor one's word, once given. The civilian focus on morality contrasts with the common law's concern for efficiency as the primary priority. The contrast between the two systems is not only pervasive but fundamental, influencing the courts' assessments of factual criteria.... .The evolution of morality as the dominant focus of civilian contract law has a long history in continental Europe. Canon law made morality the guiding principle of contract law, upholding promises even if deficient in form; ... In the seventeenth century, Pufendorf ... like the canonists, believed in natural law. Pufendorf, unlike Hobbes, but like Grotius before him and Montesquieu after him, believed that humans are naturally sociable and that peace is a natural state ... This moral conception was translated into the civil codes of Europe by making specific performance the normal remedy for breach of contract, and monetary damages the exception, in contradistinction to the common law system of monetary remedies as the norm and specific performance as the exception...." [Comparative Law, An Introduction, Vivian Grosswald Curran, Carolina Academic Press 2002 p.25–26]

B: Performance-Damages in Civil Law

La. Civ. C.

Art. 1756: An obligation is a legal relationship whereby a person, called the obligor, is bound to render a performance in favor of another, called the obligee. Performance may consist of giving, doing, or not doing something.

Art. 1983: Contracts have the effect of law for the parties.... Contracts must be performed in good faith.

Art. 1986: Upon an obligor's failure to perform an obligation to deliver a thing, or not to do an act, or to execute an instrument, the court shall grant specific performance plus damages for delay if the obligee so demands. If specific performance is impracticable, the court may allow damages to the obligee.

Upon a failure to perform an obligation that has another object, such as an obligation to do, the granting of specific performance is at the discretion of the court.

Art. 1989: Damages for delay in the performance of an obligation are owed from the time the obligor is put in default.

Other damages are owed from the time the obligor has failed to perform.

Art. 1994: An obligor is liable for the damages caused by his failure to perform a conventional obligation.

A failure to perform results from nonperformance, defective performance, or delay in performance.

Art. 1995: Damages are measured by the loss sustained by the obligee and the profit of which he has been deprived.

Art. 1996: An obligor in good faith only for the damages that were foreseeable at the time the contract was made.

Art. 1997: An obligor in bad faith is liable for all the damages, foreseeable or not, that are a direct consequence of his failure to perform..

Art. 1998: Damages for nonpecuniary loss may be recovered when the contract, because of its nature, is intended to gratify a nonpecuniary interest and, because of the circumstances surrounding the formation or the nonperformance of the contract, the obligor knew, or should have known, that his failure to perform would cause that kind of loss.

Regardless of the nature of the contract, these damages may be recovered also when the obligor intended, through his failure, to aggrieve the feelings of the obligee.

Art. 2002: An obligee must make reasonable efforts to mitigate the damage caused by the obligor's failure to perform. When an obligee fails to make these efforts, the obligor may demand that the damages be accordingly reduced.

La. C.C. P.

Art. 2504: If a judgment directs a party to perform a specific act, and he fails to comply within the time specified, the court may direct the act to be done by the sheriff or some other person appointed by the court, at the cost of the disobedient party, and with the same effect as if done by the party.

Fr. Civ .C.

Art. 1134: Conventions legally formed.... must be performed in good faith.

Art. 1136: The obligation to give carries with it the obligation to deliver the thing and to preserve it until delivery, under the penalty to have to pay damages to the creditor.

Art. 1138: The obligation to deliver is perfected by the mere exchange of consent between the contracting parties. The creditor becomes the owner of the thing ...

Art. 1142: Any obligation to do or not to do, in case of non-performance by the obligor, is transformed into an obligation to pay damages.

Art. 1144: The creditor may also, in case of non-performance, be authorized to have the obligation performed on his own at the expense of the obligor.

Art. 1146: Damages are due only after the obligor has been put in default to perform his obligation, except when the thing the obligor was bound to give or do could only be carried out within a certain time that has expired.

Art. 1149: Damages owed the obligee are, in general, in an amount equal to the loss incurred and the gain of which he has been deprived, unless one of the following exceptions apply.

Articles 1150 and 1151 of the Fr. Civ. C., see similar Articles 1996–1997 of the La. Civ. C. supra]

Fr. C.C. P.

Art. 1425-1: Performance in kind of an obligation created by a contract between two parties.... may be asked from the lower court should the value of the performance requested not exceed the amount corresponding to the court's jurisdiction.

French Legislative Act 91-650 (9 July 1991) on enforcement of civil actions.

Art. 1. Any obligee may, under the conditions laid down by legislation, compel his obligor, when the latter is at fault, to specifically perform his obligations towards the former.

Specific performance and measures of conservation cannot be aimed at persons who are protected by an exemption from performance.

Art. 2. An obligee who holds an enforceable title acknowledging a liquidated and demandable debt may proceed with its forced execution on the assets of his debtor under the conditions which govern each type of measure of execution.

BGB

Section 242. The obligor must perform in a manner consistent with good faith taking into account common usage.

Section 241. (1) By virtue of the obligation the obligee is entitled to demand performance from the obligor. The performance may also consist of an omission.

Section 249. (1) Anyone liable in damages must restore the condition that would exist if the circumstance obliging him to pay damages had not occurred.

Section 252. The damage to be compensated also comprises the lost profits. Those profits are considered lost that in the normal course of events.... could in all probability be expected.

Sw. Fed. C.O.

Art. 68: The obligor is bound to perform in person only if the obligee has an interest in having the obligation performed by the obligor himself.

Art. 97: Whenever the obligee cannot obtain performance of the obligation … the obligor must repair the damage he caused, unless he can prove that he was not at fault in not performing or not performing well.

Art. 98: When the object of an obligation is to do something, the obligee may be allowed to have the obligation performed at the expense of the obligor; the obligee may still have an action in damages.

Whenever an obligor is in breach of an obligation not to do he will owe damages by the mere fact that he breached his obligation.

C.C.Q.

Art. 1590: An obligation confers on the creditor the right to demand that the obligation be performed in full, properly and without delay.

Where the debtor fails to perform his obligation without justification on his part and he is in default, the creditor may, without prejudice to his right to the performance of the obligation in whole or in part by equivalence, (1) force specific performance of the obligation; (2) obtain,…. (3) take any other measure provided by law to enforce his right to the performance of the obligation.

Art. 1601: A creditor may, in cases which admit of it, demand that the debtor be forced to make specific performance of the obligation.

Art. 1602: In case of default, the creditor may perform the obligation or cause it to be performed at the expense of the debtor….

Art. 1607: The creditor is entitled to damages for bodily, moral or material injury which is an immediate and direct consequence of the debtor's default.

Art. 1611: The damages due to the creditor compensate for the amount of the loss he has sustained and the profit of which he has been deprived.

Future injury which is certain and able to be assessed is taken into account in awarding damages.

Art. 1613: In contractual matters, the debtor is liable only for damages that were foreseen or foreseeable at the time the obligation was contracted, where the failure to perform the obligation does not proceed from intentional or gross fault on his part; even then, the damages include only what is an immediate and direct consequence of the nonperformance.

[The Italian Civil Code: see, for example: Articles 1218, 1223, 1225]

Philippe Malaurie, Laurent Aynès, Philippe Stoffel-Munck
Les Obligations, Defrénois 2003 p.594 et seq.

§ 1. Specific performance of Obligations in kind

1.-Direct constraint

[...] English law does grant specific performance only in exceptional cases, because, in general, it infringes upon individual freedom.

On account of the difficulties raised by specific performance by means of direct constraint, French law devised different measures of indirect constraint, the only surviving one being 'astreinte'(a daily penalty for delay in performing)

1129 [...], In reality, it is impossible to have an obligation to do specifically enforced by public authorities, for fear of satisfying the private interest of the creditor at the expense of the debtor's freedom. It is only in the case of the transfer of ownership of a thing that the creditor may obtain specific performance by constraint: seize a movable, expulsion from a building ... In other cases, the creditor may be allowed to perform himself at the expense of the debtor ... (see Civ. C. art 1144) ... which suggests that the obligation is not *intuitus personae*.

1130 [Civ. C. Art.1142], this text is an application of the rule *nemo precise cogi ad factum* (which) protects one's individual freedom.... Specific performance in kind is denied today when it would offend a moral, material or legal impossibility. Either because of the personal nature of the obligation; thus, one could not specifically and forcefully compel an artist to carry out his obligation (a painting, for instance); or because one would face too many and major material obstacles; or because of a legal impossibility to enforce the obligation which would not otherwise prevent an 'equivalent' performance (damages, for example).

1131 [...] Anytime an obligation to do can be enforced by constraint, performance in kind must be ordered. Thus, a buyer should be compelled to take delivery of the thing sold to him and delivered by the seller;..a tenant who refuses to leave the premises at the end of the lease can be expelled; ...

2.-Astreinte

1132. **Indirect but effective.** -Astreinte ... targets the debtor's wallet to compel him to perform. Astreinte has for its purpose the execution of a judicial

7 · PERFORMANCE-DAMAGES   133

decision of which it is the accessory; the judge can, even of his own motion, sentence the debtor to pay a sum of money, for each day of delay in general; it is, therefore, in the interest of the debtor to perform as soon as possible.... Astreinte is 'personal' to the debtor in the sense that the debtor cannot pass it on to his sureties.

1134. Scope of application. Almost any court decision can have an astreinte attached to it, even when the object of the obligation is tainted with *intuitus personae* ... However very strictly personal obligations, such as an artist's obligation, cannot be enforced by way of an astreinte. (a capricious artist would act poorly under any constraint ... ; damages are a better remedy..)

1135.[...]..Astreinte is different from damages and has for its main purpose to 'crush' the obligor's resistance to the court's decision; it is a kind of *contempt of Court.*

C. Performance-Damages in Common Law

Restatement, 2d

§ 235. Effect of Performance as Discharge and of Non-Performance as Breach

(1) Full performance of a duty under a contract discharges the duty.

(2) When performance of a duty under a contract is due any non-performance is a breach.

§ 236. Claims for Damages for Total and for Partial Breach

(1) A claim for damages for total breach is one for damages based on all of the injured party's remaining rights to performance.

(2) A claim for damages for partial breach is one for damages based on only part of the injured party's remaining rights to performance.

§ 243. Effect of a Breach by Non-Performance as Giving Rise to a Claim for Damages for Total Breach

(1) With respect to performances to be exchanged under an exchange of promises, a breach by non-performance gives rise to a claim for damages for total breach only if it discharges the injured party's remaining duties to render such performance, other than a duty to render an agreed equivalent under § 240.

(2) Except as stated in Subsection (3), a breach by non-performance accompanied or followed by a repudiation gives rise to a claim for damages for total breach.

(3) Where at the time of the breach the only remaining duties of performance are those of the party in breach and are for the payment of money in installments not related to one another, his breach by non-performance as to less than the whole, whether or not accompanied or followed by a repudiation, does not give rise to a claim for damages for total breach.

(4) In any case other than those stated in the preceding subsections, a breach by non-performance gives rise to a claim for total breach only if it so substantially impairs the value of the contract to the injured party at the time of the breach that it is just in the circumstances to allow him to recover damages based on all his remaining rights to performance.

UCC

§ 2-503. Manner of Seller's Tender of Delivery.

(1) Tender of delivery requires that the seller put and hold conforming goods at the buyer's disposition and give the buyer any notification reasonably necessary to enable him to take delivery. The manner, time and place for tender are determined by the agreement and this Article, …

§ 2-511. Tender of Payment by Buyer; Payment by Check.

(1) Unless otherwise agreed tender of payment is a condition to the seller's duty to tender and complete any delivery.

§ 2-703. Seller's Remedies in General.

(1) A breach of contract by the buyer includes the buyer's wrongful rejection or wrongful attempt to revoke acceptance of goods, wrongful failure to perform a contractual obligation, failure to make a payment when due, and repudiation.

(2) If the buyer is in breach of contract the seller, to the extent provided for by this Act or other law, may:

(a) withhold delivery of such goods;

(h) recover damages for nonacceptance or repudiation under Section 2-708(1);

(i) recover lost profits ...

(k) obtain specific performance under Section 2-716;

(m) in other cases, recover damages in any manner that is reasonable under the circumstances.

§ 2-713. Buyer's Damages for Nondelivery or Repudiation.

(1) Subject to Section 2-723, wrongfully fails to deliver or repudiates or the buyer rightfully rejects or justifiably revokes acceptance:

(a) the measure of damages.... .is the difference between the market price at the time for tender under the contract and the contract price together with incidental or consequential damages.... but less expenses saved in consequence of the seller's breach; and

(b)   the measure of damages for repudiation by the seller is the difference between the market price at the expiration of a commercially reasonable time after the buyer learned of the repudiation.... .and the contract price together with any incidental or consequential damages....

§ 2-714. Buyer's Damages For Breach in Regard to Accepted Goods.

(1) The measure of damages for breach of warranty is the difference at the time an place of acceptance between the value of the goods accepted and the value they would have had if they had been as warranted, ...

§ 2-716. Specific Performance; Buyer's Right of Replevin.

(1) Specific performance may be decreed if the goods are unique or in other proper circumstances. In a contract other than a consumer contract, specific performance may be decreed if the parties have agreed to that remedy. However, even if the parties agree to specific performance, specific performance may not be decreed if the breaching party's sole remaining contractual obligation is the payment of money.

(2) The decree for specific performance may include such terms and conditions as to payment of the price, damages, or other relief as the court may deem just.

(3) The buyer has a right of replevin or similar remedy for goods identified to the contract if after reasonable effort the buyer is unable to effect cover for such goods or the circumstances reasonably indicate that such effort will be unavailing or if the goods have been shipped under reservation and satisfaction of the security interest in them has been made or tendered.

(4) ...

G.H. Treitel, Q.C.
(opus cited)

SECTION 3: RESCISSION FOR FAILURE TO PERFORM

1. Introduction

(1) Terminology

Failure to perform may (and often will) amount to breach of contract. Where this is the case it will give rise to the usual remedies for breach of contract, such as actions for damages, for an agreed sum or for specific relief.

CHAPTER 19. BREACH

SECTION 1. WHAT AMOUNTS TO BREACH

A breach of contract is committed when a party without lawful excuse fails or refuses to perform what is due from him under the contract, performs defectively or incapacitates himself from performing.

SECTION 2. EFFECTS OF BREACH

A breach of contract may entitle the injured party to claim damages, the agreed sum, specific performance or an injunction, in accordance with the principles discussed ... In appropriate circumstances he may be entitled to more than one of these remedies: e.g. to an injunction and damages....

CHAPTER 21 REMEDIES

A breach of contract is a civil wrong. To break a contract can also occasionally be a criminal offence; ... In most cases, however, a breach of contract will involve only civil liability;.... .A claim for specific relief is one for the actual performance of the defaulting party's undertaking. Where that undertaking is one to do, or to forbear from doing, some act, a claim for specific relief is made by the equitable remedies of specific performance or injunction; where the undertaking is one to pay a sum of money, a claim for specific relief is made by the common law action for an agreed sum. In an action for damages, the injured party claims compensation in money for the fact that he has not received the performance for which he bargained ... A person who has performed his part of the contract but has not received the agreed counter-performance may, finally, claim back his performance or its reasonable value ...

SECTION 1. DAMAGES

The action for damages is always available, as of right, when a contract has been broken. It should, from this point of view, be contrasted with claims for specific relief and for restitution, which are either subject to the discretion of the court or only available if certain conditions are satisfied. An action for damages can succeed even though the victim has not suffered any loss: in that event, it will result in an award of nominal damages. In such a case, the purpose of the action may simply be to establish what the rights and liabilities of the parties under a contract are ... Generally the victim will claim damages for a substantial loss; ...

(2) Compensation for what?

The principle that damages are compensatory naturally gives rise to the question: for what is it that the victim of a breach of contract is entitled to be compensated? This question calls for an analysis of the various types of losses for which the victim of a breach of contract can recover damages;..

(a) *Loss of bargain.*[...]..the plaintiff is entitled to be compensated for the loss of his bargain, so that his expectations arising out of or created by the contract are protected....

(b) *Reliance loss.* An alternative principle is to put the plaintiff into the position in which he would have been if the contract had never been made by compensating him for expenses incurred (or other loss suffered) in reliance on the contract ...

(c) *Restitution.*

(e) *Incidental and consequential loss.* The victim of a breach of contract can often recover loss which does not fit easily into the categories so far discussed. First, he may incur expenses after a breach has come to his attention,.... Second, the injured party may suffer "consequential" loss. (loss of profits; reliance loss; further harm, such as personal injury or damage to property, suffered as a result of breach;..

SECTION 3. EQUITABLE REMEDIES

1. Specific performance

The common law did not specifically enforce contractual obligations except those to pay money. Specific enforcement of other contractual obligations was available only in equity. It was (and is) subject to many restrictions. These are based partly on the drastic character of the remedy, which leads (more readily than an award of damages or of the agreed sum) to attachment of the defendant's person. But this is an important factor only where the contract calls for "personal" performance, *i.e.* for acts to be done by the defendant himself. Where the contract is not of this kind, it can be specifically enforced without personal constraint: for example, by sequestration, by execution of a formal document by an officer of the court, or by a writ of delivery ... The more recent authorities ... support some expansion in the scope of the remedy.

(1) Granted where damages not "adequate"

The traditional view is that specific performance will not be ordered where damages are an "adequate" remedy....

(a) *Availability of satisfactory equivalent.* Damages are most obviously an adequate remedy where the plaintiff can get a satisfactory equivalent of what he contracted for from some other choice. For this reason specific performance is not generally ordered of contracts for the sale of commodities, or of shares, which are readily available in the market. In such cases the plaintiff can buy in the market and is adequately compensated by recovering the difference between the contract and the market price by way of damages.

Damages will, on the other hand, not be regarded as an adequate remedy where the plaintiff cannot obtain a satisfactory substitute. The law takes the view that a buyer of land or of a house (however ordinary) is not adequately compensated by damages, and that he can therefore get an order of specific performance ... A vendor of land, ... can get specific performance, though his only claim is for money. One reason for this is that it is just to allow the remedy *to* him as it is available *against* him. Another is that damages will not adequately compensate him for not getting the whole price, as he may not easily be able to find another purchaser.... [T]he rule seems to apply though the land is readily saleable to a third party;

(c) *Damages hard to quantify.* A second factor that is relevant (though not decisive) in considering the adequacy of damages is the difficulty of assessing and recovering them. This is one reason why specific performance has been ordered of contracts to sell(or to pay) annuities ...

(e) *Appropriateness of the remedy.* The more satisfactory approach found in the cases just discussed is also expressed in dicta to the effect that the availability of specific performance depends on the *appropriateness* of that remedy in the circumstances of each case. The question is not simply whether damages are an "adequate" remedy, but whether specific performance will "do more perfect and complete justice than an award of damages." ...

(2) Discretionary

Specific performance is a discretionary remedy: the court is not bound to grant it merely because the contract is valid at law and cannot be impeached on some specific equitable ground such as misrepresentation or undue influence ... The discretion is, however, "not an arbitrary ... discretion, but one to be governed as far as possible by fixed rules and principles."

(a) *Severe hardship.* Specific performance can be refused on the ground of severe hardship to the defendant.

(b) *Unfairness.* The court can refuse specific performance of a contract which has been obtained by means that are unfair, ...

(c) *Inadequacy of consideration* ...

(d) *Conduct of plaintiff.* "The conduct of the party applying for relief is always an important element for consideration."

(3) Contracts not specifically enforceable

(a) *Contracts involving personal service.* It has long been settled that equity will not, as a general rule, enforce a contract of personal service.... The equitable principle applies to all contracts involving personal service even though they are not strictly contracts of service ... The equitable principle of refusing specific performance is limited to contracts for services of a personal nature ... Thus specific performance can be ordered of a contract to publish a piece of music and sometimes of contracts to build ...

(b) *Contracts requiring constant supervision.* Specific performance will not be ordered of continuous contractual duties ...

2. Injunction

(1) General

The court can sometimes restrain a party by injunction from committing a breach of contract. The remedy is most appropriate where the contract is negative in nature or contains a negative stipulation ...

Butterworths

(opus cited)

Overview

8.1 Breach of contract is a legal wrong for which the civil law provides a remedy. The principal judicial remedy is an award of unliquidated damages. Unliquidated damages are damages which are assessed by the court as appropriate to be paid to the victim of a breach of contract in respect of his or, exceptionally, others' losses caused by the breach. Damages for breach of contract generally seek to compensate the victim for his loss rather than to punish the wrongdoer for his conduct. The general compensatory aim means that in the absence of provable loss only nominal damages will be awarded.[...]

Liquidated damages clauses are terms of a contract which stipulate for the payment of a sum of money by a contracting party in the event of the payer's breach. Such clauses are said to be unenforceable if they require the payment of a 'penalty' i.e. a sum in excess of a genuine pre-estimate of loss.

Specific performance

Nature of remedy

8.155 Specific performance grew out of petitions to the Chancellor in his Court in Chancery to require someone to do the very thing he had promised. Most cases involved agreements to sell land but various other promises were enforced as well. The jurisdiction is therefore an equitable one with the consequence that the remedy is not available as of right but rather as the discretion of the court. This discretion is now exercised to deny the remedy when certain 'bars' arise. The most important of these bars is that damages are an adequate remedy. [...] The various prohibitions and limits upon the availability of the remedies of specific enforcement and injunction, particularly the bar that damages must be an inadequate remedy, are less restrictive than they were in the past: 'a court is not in modern times perhaps so constrained as once it was by black letter rules.' [...]

E. Allan Farnsworth
(opus cited)

Chapter 8 Performance and Nonperformance

A. PERFORMANCE IN GENERAL

§ 8.1. Goals and concepts.[..] When parties make a bilateral contract, they exchange promises in the expectation of a subsequent exchange of performances.... The principal goal of the rules applicable to the performance stage of such contracts is to protect that expectation against a possible failure of the other party to perform. It would be possible, of course, to leave a party who has not received the expected performance to pursue a claim for damages. But the injured party bargained for performance rather than for a lawsuit. Therefore courts have developed rules to afford the injured party, in addition to any claim for damages, a variety of types of self-help, the most important of which is the right to suspend its own performance and ultimately to refuse to perform if the other party fails to perform.

C. NONPERFORMANCE

§ 8.9. Constructive Conditions of Exchange. [...] Since a bilateral contract involves an exchange of promises and the performance of each is made a condition of the duty to perform the other, such implied conditions are often called *constructive conditions of exchange.*

Constructive conditions of exchange play an essential role in assuring the parties to a bilateral contract that they will actually receive the performance that they have been promised.[...] Courts sometimes speak confusingly ... of "failure of consideration" when what is meant is failure of performance.

§ 8 12. Substantial Performance as a Means of Avoiding Forfeiture.[...] A factor of special importance in assessing the impact of a breach on the injured party's expectations is the extent to which that party can be compensated adequately in damages ...

Chapter 12

REMEDIES

A. CONTRACT REMEDIES IN GENERAL

§ 12.1. Purpose of Remedies. Why do people keep their promises? ... Our system of contract remedies is not directed at *compulsion of promisors to pre-*

vent breach; it is aimed, instead, at *relief to promisees* to *redress* breach. Its preoccupation is not with the question: how can promisors be made to keep promises? Its concern is with a different question: how can people be encouraged to deal with those who make promises? ... Perhaps it is more consistent with free enterprise to promote the use of contract by encouraging promises to rely on the promises of others instead of by compelling promisors to perform their promises. In any event, along with the celebrated freedom to make contracts goes a considerable freedom to break them as well.

How do courts encourage promises to rely on promises? Ordinarily they do so by protecting the expectation that the injured party had when making the contract by attempting to put that party in as good a position as it would have been in had the contract been performed, that is, had there been no breach. The interest measured in this way is called the *expectation interest* and is said to give the injured party the "benefit of the bargain." The expectation interest is based ... on the actual value that the contract would have had to the injured party had it been performed.

At times, a court will enforce a promise by protecting the promisee's reliance instead of the promisee's expectation. The injured party may ... have changed position in reliance on the contract by incurring expenses in preparation or in performance ... [t]he court may attempt to put the injured party back in the position in which that party would have been had the contract not been made. The interest measured in this way is called the *reliance interest*.

§ 12.2. Types of Remedies. The judicial remedies available for breach of contract can be characterized as "specific" or "substitutional." Relief is said to be specific when it is intended to give the injured party the very performance that was promised, as when the court orders a defaulting seller of goods to deliver them to the buyer. Relief is said to be substitutional when it is intended to give the promise something in substitution for the promised performance, as when the court awards a buyer of goods money damages instead of the goods.

Judicial remedies for breach of contract can also be characterized as either "legal" or "equitable," depending on whether, before the merger of law and equity, they were available in the common law courts or in courts of equity. The principal legal remedy to enforce a promise is a judgment awarding a sum of money. This is usually substitutional relief ... The principal equitable remedy to enforce a contract is an order requiring specific performance of the contract or enjoining its nonperformance. This is specific relief.

B. ENFORCEMENT BY SPECIFIC PERFORMANCE AND INJUNCTION

§ 12.4. Historical Development of Equitable Relief. [...] The common law courts did not generally grant specific relief for breach of contract. The usual form of relief at common law was substitutional, and the typical judgment declared that the plaintiff recover from the defendant a sum of money ...

§ 12.5. Forms: Specific Performance and Injunction. The most direct form of equitable relief for breach of contract is specific performance ... A court will not order a performance that has become impossible, unreasonably burdensome, or unlawful, nor will is issue an order that can be frustrated by the defendant through exercise of a power of termination or otherwise. Specific performance may be granted after there has been a breach of contract by either nonperformance or repudiation.

Instead of ordering specific performance, a court may, by injunction, direct a party to refrain from doing a specified act.... A claimant who sues for specific performance or an injunction and is denied that relief may be awarded damages or restitution in the same proceeding.

C. ENFORCEMENT BY AWARD OF DAMAGES

§ 12.8. Basic Principles of Damages. The award of damages is the common form of relief for breach of contract. Virtually any breach gives the injured party a claim for damages for at least nominal damages, "to which," as a distinguished federal judge put it "for reasons we do not understand every victim of a breach of contract, unlike a tort victim, is entitled." Thus, even if the breach caused no loss.... , the injured party can recover as damages a nominal sum, commonly six cents or a dollar, fixed without regard to loss ... In most successful actions for breach of contract, however, substantial damages are awarded.

The basic principle for the measurement of those damages is that of compensation based on the injured party's expectation ... At least in principle, a party's expectation is measured by the actual worth that performance of the contract would have had to that party, not the worth that it might have had to some hypothetical person ...

[...] [a] court will not ordinarily award damages that are described as "punitive," intended to punish the party in breach, or sometimes as "exemplary," intended to make an example of that party ... Punitive damages may, however, be awarded in tort actions, and a number of courts have awarded them for a breach of contract that is in some respect tortious ...

D. Performance-Damages in International/Multinational Law

UNIDROIT

Article 5.1.4 (Duty to achieve a specific result, Duty of best efforts)

(1) To the extent that an obligation of a party involves a duty to achieve a specific result, that party is bound to achieve that result.

(2) To the extent that an obligation of a party involves a duty of best efforts in the performance of an activity, that party is bound to make such efforts as would be made by a reasonable person of the same kind in the same circumstances.

Article 7.2.1 (Performance of monetary obligations)

Where a party who is obliged to pay money does not do so, the other party may require payment.

Article 7.2.2 (Performance of non-monetary obligation)

Where a party who owes an obligation other than one to pay money does not perform, the other party may require performance, unless

(a) to (e)

Article 7.2.4 (Judicial penalty)

(1) Where the court orders a party to perform, it may also direct that this party pay a penalty if it does not comply with the order.

(2) The penalty shall be paid to the aggrieved party unless mandatory provisions of the law of the forum provide otherwise. Payment of the penalty to the aggrieved party does not exclude any claim for damages.

Article 7.2.5 (Change of remedy)

(1) An aggrieved party who has required performance of a non-monetary obligation.... may invoke any other remedy.

(2) Where the decision of a court for performance of a non-monetary obligation cannot be enforced, the aggrieved party may invoke any other remedy.

Article 7.4.2 (Full compensation)

(1) The aggrieved party is entitled to full compensation for harm sustained as a result of the non-performance. Such harm includes both

any loss which it suffered and any gain of which it was deprived, taking into account any gain to the aggrieved party resulting from its avoidance of cost or harm.

(2) Such harm may be non-pecuniary and includes, for instance, physical suffering or emotional distress.

Article 7.4.4 (Foreseeability of harm)

The non-performing party is liable only for harm which it foresaw or could reasonably have foreseen at the time of the conclusion of the contract as being likely to result from its non-performance.

Principles of European Contract Law

Article 8:102: Cumulation of Remedies

Remedies which are not incompatible may be cumulated. In particular, a party is not deprived of its right to damages by exercising its right to any other remedy.

Article 9:102:Non-monetary Obligations

(1) The aggrieved party is entitled to specific performance of an obligation other than one to pay money, including the remedying of a defective performance.

(2) Specific performance cannot, however, be obtained where:

(a) performance would be unlawful or impossible; or

(b) performance would cause the debtor unreasonable effort or expense; or

(c) the performance consists in the provision of services or work of a personal character or depends upon a personal relationship, or

(d) the aggrieved party may reasonably obtain performance from another source.

(3) The aggrieved party will lose the right to specific performance if it fails to seek it within a reasonable time after it has or ought to have become aware of the non-performance.

Article 9: 502: General Measure of Damages

The general measure of damages is such sum as will put the aggrieved party as nearly as possible into the position in which it would have been if the contract had been duly performed. Such damages cover the loss which the aggrieved party has suffered and the gain of which it has been deprived.

Article 9:503: Foreseeability

The non-performing party is liable only for loss which it foresaw or could reasonably have foreseen at the time of conclusion of the contract as a likely result of its non-performance, unless the non-performance was intentional or grossly negligent.

CISG

Article 25

A breach of contract committed by one of the parties is fundamental if it results in such detriment to the other party as substantially to deprive him of what he is entitled to expect under the contract, unless the party in breach did not foresee and a reasonable person of the same kind in the same circumstances would not have foreseen such a result.

Article 28

If, in accordance with the provisions of this Convention, one party is entitled to require performance of any obligation by the other party, a court is not bound to enter a judgment for specific performance unless the court would do so under its own law in respect of similar contracts of sale not governed by this Convention

Article 46

(1) The buyer may require performance by the seller of his obligations unless the buyer has resorted to a remedy which is inconsistent with this requirement.

(2) If the goods do not conform with the contract, the buyer may require delivery of substitute goods only if the lack of conformity constitutes a fundamental breach of contract and a request for substitute goods is made either in conjunction with notice given under article 39 or within a reasonable time thereafter.

(3) If the goods do not conform with the contract, the buyer may require the seller to remedy the lack of conformity by repair, unless this is unreasonable having regard to all the circumstances. A request for repair must be made either in conjunction with notice given under article 39 or within a reasonable time thereafter.

Article 62

The seller may require the buyer to pay the price, take delivery or perform his other obligations, unless the seller has resorted to a remedy which is inconsistent with this requirement.

Article 74
Damages for breach of contract by one party consist of a sum equal to the loss, including loss of profit, suffered by the other party as a consequence of the breach. Such damages may not exceed the loss which the party in breach foresaw or ought to have foreseen at the time of the conclusion of the contract, in the light of the facts and matters of which he then knew or ought to have known, as a possible consequence of the breach of contract.

E. Courts' Decisions

1. Civil Law

Louisiana
J. Weingarten, Inc. v. Northgate Mall, Inc.
404 So. 2d 896, 1981 [Supreme Court of Louisiana]

DENNIS, Justice.

We are called upon to decide whether, under the circumstances of this case, a court should specifically enforce a lease by ordering the destruction of the major part of a $4 million building which a shopping center developer erected in an area reserved to its tenant for customer parking. The trial court refused to order the building razed, but the court of appeal reversed, requiring that approximately 60% of the building be torn down and removed within six months of the effective date of its judgment.[...]

Pursuant to plaintiff's petition, the trial court issued a temporary restraining order prohibiting further construction activities and continued the order until March 19, 1979 when a hearing was held on plaintiff's motion to dissolve the restraining order. The trial court denied the preliminary injunction and dissolved the temporary restraining order based on its finding that Weingarten failed to show that it would sustain irreparable damage without injunctive relief.[...]

The trial on the merits of the petition for a permanent injunction was not held until October 25 and 26, 1979. By this time the $4 million expansion project was virtually complete and the new stores therein were open for business.

After the trial on the permanent injunction, the trial court reaffirmed its earlier finding that the plaintiff had not demonstrated that it would be irreparably harmed and could be adequately compensated monetarily. The court refused to enforce specifically a provision in the lease stipulating that an injunction to enforce Weingarten's rights to egress and passage over the parking area occupied by the new building could be obtained without the necessity of showing irreparable harm or the inadequacy of damages. The trial court concluded the agreed remedy provision was against public policy[...]

The court of appeal reversed the trial court, holding that the plaintiff was entitled to permanent injunctive relief because the agreed remedy provision was valid and because the plaintiff was irreparably harmed.[...]

The decisive issue presented by the breaches of contract is whether Weingarten is entitled to the substantive right of specific performance under the circumstances of this case. Specific performance may be enforced by the extraordinary remedy of injunction, among other procedural methods. [...] unless Weingarten has a substantive right to specifically enforce the obligation, neither an injunction nor any other procedural remedy may be used. [...]

Plaintiff Weingarten has asked specific performance of defendant Northgate's obligation not to do something namely, not to infringe on plaintiff's contractual rights over areas reserved for parking by the lease. Civil Code articles 1926 through 1929 govern the enforcement of obligations to do, or not to do.[...]

[1]Articles 1926 through 1929 were intended to give first rank to the obligee's right to performance in specific form, consistently with other provisions of the Code. [...]Therefore, we reject the common law view that the obligee must first clear the inadequacy of damage-irreparable injury hurdle before invoking the remedy.[...]

A reading of the articles as a whole, however, implies that courts are empowered to withhold specific performance in some exceptional cases even when specific performance is possible.[...] The civil law systems, i.e., those descended from Roman law, have by and large proceeded on the premise that specific redress should be ordered whenever possible, unless disadvantages of the remedy outweigh its advantages.[...] The main reservations have been for cases where specific relief is impossible, would involve disproportionate cost, would introduce compulsion into close personal relationships or compel the expression of special forms of artistic or intellectual creativity.[...]

[2] [...] we conclude that the legislative aim of the redactors of the code was to institute the right to specific performance as an obligee's remedy for breach of contract except when it is impossible, greatly disproportionate in cost to the actual damage caused, no longer in the creditor's interest, or of substantial negative effect upon the interests of third parties. [...]

[3] Although the contractual provisions involved here cannot be specifically enforced under the circumstances of this case, we hold that they could have been under different conditions. Indeed, unless exceptional conditions prevail as in this case anything which has been done in violation of the contract may be undone, including the destruction of a building. Moreover, plaintiff is not without a remedy because it is entitled to be compensated fully in damages for any loss it sustains as a result of the breach of contract.[...]

France

Cass.-civ. March 14, 1900
S.1900 I 189

The Court: Considering that the convention by which a painter binds himself to paint a portrait, for a set price, is a contract of a special nature, in such a way that the ownership of the painting is not definitively acquired by the party who ordered it until the artist placed the painting at the disposal of that party and until that party has approved that painting; until then the painter remains in full control of his work, ... ; in case of failure by the artist to comply with his commitment, he will be held liable to pay damages; Considering that Whistler bound himself to paint Lady Eden's portrait, but that he constantly refused to actually deliver the painting to the possession of the plaintiff who had ordered it; that after having exhibited the painting in the Champ-de-Mars gallery, he proceeded with making some drastic changes to the painting, replacing Lady Eden' head with another person's head; ... [The Cour de Cassation held that the plaintiff had not become owner of the painting and, thus, could not ask for its delivery; that Whistler had to pay damages, return the down payment received and was forbidden to make any use of the painting until it was so modified that it could no longer be identified ...]

Cass.-civ. Jan. 16, 2007
D.2007 Notes no 16 p.1119

The Court: Considering Articles 1134 and 1142 of the civil Code, Articles 4 and 12 together of the New Code of civil procedure; -Considering that the party vis-à-vis whom a contractual commitment has not been performed has the right to specifically compel the other party to perform the convention whenever it is possible; ... Considering that by contract of Fev. 7, 2005, the corporation Michel Lafon publishing transferred to the corporation Librairie

générale française (LGF) the right to commercialize in the collection "Livre
de Poche," for a term of 5 years, the work of Ian X ... and Dustin Y ... called
" La règle de quatre," denying itself, for the duration of the contract, the possibility to publish or allow the publication of that work in a widely distributed collection with a sale price that would not be at least two and a half
times superior to the price of the collection "de poche"; considering that,
having learned that despite its commitments Michel Lafon was about to
commercialize the work in a collection with a price not exceeding 10 euros,
LGF sued Michel Lafon 'en référé' to have it prohibited, under astreinte to
engage in acts of commercialization and to have it withdraw from any sale
copies of the work already available on the market; ... ; considering that the
decision of the Court of Appeal here challenged ruled that when prohibiting
Michel Lafon to continue to commercialize the work in litigation, whereas
according to article 1142 of the civil code any obligation to do or not to do is
transformed into an obligation to pay damages, in case of non performance
of its obligation by the obligor.... the judges of the lower court had acted beyond their power and failed to take into consideration the articles cited;....
[considering] that, thereby,...,when LGF was only making use of the right
granted any contracting party to ask for specific performance of the convention whenever it is possible, ... the Court of Appeal did violate article 1142
of the civil code when it misapplied it and when it failed to apply other
texts ...

For these reasons, the decision of the Court of Appeal is quashed ...

Québec

La Compagnie de Construction Belcourt Ltée c. Golden Griddle Pancake House Limited

[1988] R.J.Q. 716 to 729

Cour Supérieure:

[Facts: The plaintiffs (Belcourt/Renary) are owners of a farmer's market
shopping centre[...] known as Les Halles d'Anjou (Les Halles). Defendant.
Golden Griddle Pancake House Limited (Golden Griddle). [...] leased
premises for the operation of a restaurant in Les Halles. Golden Griddle had
entered into a franchise agreement on August 12th, 1985, with Messrs.
Sunny Banh and Henry Au Yeung, and in pursuance of that franchise agreement subleased the premises to Messrs. Banh and Au Yeung, who, in turn,
transferred their rights under the lease, the sublease and the franchise agreement to 146585 Canada Inc. After the restaurant was completed and open

for business, the volume of business generated was insufficient and as a consequence 146585 Canada Inc. made an assignment in bankruptcy. When this case was heard, the restaurant had been closed for several months. Belcourt/Renary by its action seeks the sum of 40 366,36 $ representing arrears of base rental, tax recoveries, common area charges and promotion fund only for the months of July, August, September and October 1987, as well as a permanent injunction to compel Golden Griddle to reopen the restaurant and to operate it in a complete and continuous fashion as required under the terms of the lease.]

An injunction must be distinguished from other remedies available to the creditor of an obligation because it is an equitable remedy. It imposes a duty, the violation of which constitutes contempt of court. A stipulation in an agreement by the debtor that his creditor may obtain injunctive relief upon the occurrence of a default does not automatically create a right to such remedy. It is therefore necessary to review the circumstances in which the law provides for the issue of an injunction as a means of obtaining specific performance of an obligation and determine their applicability to the case at bar. [...]

The consequence of a failure to respect an obligation is set forth in Article 1065 C.C. which provides the following:

> Art. 1065. Every obligation renders the debtor liable in damages in case of a breach of it on his part. The creditor may, *in cases which admit of it*, demand also a specific performance of the obligation, and that he be authorized to execute it at the debtor's expense, or that the contract from which the obligation arises be set aside; subject to the special provisions contained in this Code, and without prejudice, in either case, to his claim for damages.
>
> [...]

The language of the Code is clear. It provides the creditor of the obligation with the right, *at his option*, to require specific performance of the obligation, subject only to the qualification that the situation be one of the "cases which admit of it." It is not the role of the Court to select or predetermine the creditor's recourse, but rather to respond to his election.

There are three distinct types of specific performance:

1) The substitution of a judgment of the Court for an act of the debtor.[...]

2) The substitution of the act of creditor for that of the debtor. [...]

3) Compulsion of the debtor by Court order to perform a positive obligation he has undertaken to do, or cease doing that which he has undertaken not to do. [...]

It is settled law that the parties to a lease are entitled to demand specific performance in the appropriate cases. [...]

Cases which do not admit of specific performance are usually situations where the performance of the obligation has become virtually impossible, when the time within which the obligation was to be performed has elapsed, or the property to be delivered has perished or is no longer in the patrimony of the debtor of the obligation.[...]

Where specific performance could only be obtained by judicial compulsion of the debtor of the obligation to perform a positive obligation, the courts have been reluctant, event recalcitrant to compel compliance with the obligation and preferred to award damages in these circumstances.[...]

It was established that Golden Griddle was one of the three large restaurants in the centre. Although the other two have enjoyed substantial sales volumes, the closure of Golden griddle will affect the atmosphere of the centre and sales by other tenants. Golden Griddle cannot obtain relief from its obligation to operate on the grounds that it had failed to generate a satisfactory level of sales.[...]

Golden griddle invokes the doctrine of hardship asserting that the reopening and operation of its restaurant would necessitate the expenditure of hundreds of thousands of dollars without commensurate benefit to Belcourt/Renary.[...]

In the case at bar, Golden griddle was fully aware of the cost of opening and operating a restaurant when it signed the offer to lease and the lease. Third parties' rights will not be adversely affected by the issue of an injunction. Undoubtedly the Defendant will be obliged to expend considerable funds to reopen the restaurant and may be obliged to subsidize its operations. These were readily foreseeable consequences at the time Golden Griddle contracted its obligations under the lease and are commensurate with the rewards to be earned if the restaurant's operations are successful. It is specious to suggest that courts should refrain from enforcing contracts if the defendant will lose money as a consequence. Judicial intervention is rarely necessary to enforce contracts which will yield a profit to the defendant.[...]

[...]the Court:

[...]

Issues a permanent injunction ordering the Defendant, within 60 days following the service of this judgment, to reopen to the public its Golden griddle restaurant in the premises leased by Defendant from Plaintiff in Les

Halles d'Anjou, and thereafter, during the pendency of its lease for these premises, a) to operate such restaurant in the entire leased premises continuously during the normal business hours of Les Halles d'Anjou; and b)to maintain therein restaurant services[...] at a level that shall not be less than the average level of these services in the Golden griddle restaurant in Les Halles d'Anjou during the month of May 1987;

Condemns the Defendant to pay to Plaintiff the sum of 40 366,36 $, representing arrears of base rental, tax recoveries, common area changes and promotion fund only, for the months of July, August, September and October 1987, inclusive, with interest at the rate of 16% from the due date of such arrears;[...]

Association des Professeurs de Lignery (A.P.L.), Syndicat Affilié à la C.E.Q. c. Florence Alvetta-Comeau
[1990] R.J.Q. 130 to 138.

Cour d'Appel : M. le Juge BAUDOUIN

[Facts omitted : only issue of exemplary damages addressed here]

3. Exemplary damages

Exemplary damages exist, in the civil law of Québec, only exceptionally. Such is the case of the legislative act on the protection of trees; the legislative act on consumer protection;.... and, of course, the Charte des droits et libertés de la personne (Charter of Human Rights and Freedoms)....

Exemplary damages can be granted only if two requirements are met: illegality of the infringement and its intentional occurrence ...

Exemplary damages come to us from the common law wherein they have a long history. Integrated into our civil law, they must find a space and an interpretation compatible with the principles and the rules of the civil law. Their aim is not to compensate for a loss or a failed profit. They actually do not have any compensatory function. Their objective is dual: first of all, they are meant to penalize the behavior of the perpetrator of an act considered reprehensible; in the second place, they are meant to display a public reprobation towards such a behavior. It is therefore easy to understand that the granting of such damages be available in instances of violation of the fundamental rights and freedoms protected by the Charte/Charter, since some of these violations do cause only minimal material losses or moral distress. Exemplary damages allow, therefore, for a more effective public sanction.

Germany

BGH NJW 1977, 35, VIII Civil Senate

(engl. translation) in the web site of
The University of Texas School of Law[31]

Facts

In September 1967 the plaintiff, who had often done business with the defendant before, ordered from him 4 million flowerpots for the 1967–68 season. In December 1967 and on several occasions thereafter the defendant informed the plaintiff that it would not be able to supply all four million pots within the time allowed. Although the plaintiff continued to insist on timeous delivery, the defendant unilaterally decided to ration his output, and delivered only 600,000 pots in all.

The plaintiff claimed damages for the harm due to the defendant's failure to adhere to the terms of delivery. The Landgericht allowed the claim, but the Oberlandesgericht rejected it. The defendant appealed, and the decision of the Landgericht was reinstated.

Reasons

III. [...]

1. The contract of September 1967 is a contract for delivery in instalments, the agreement being for the remunerated delivery of fungible goods in instalments determined by quantity and type. Notwithstanding that delivery is agreed to take place in successive portions, such a contract is a single contract, if the parties envisage the contractual content as a whole. This is evidently what the court below assumed.

[...]

3. a) This court has held that where there is a long-term contract for instalment deliveries based on a relationship of mutual reliance the buyer can, if the seller's faulty conduct seriously imperils the purpose of the contract and its smooth operation, withdraw from further performance on the ground of positive breach of contract [references].

---

31. http://www.utexas.edu/law/academics/centers/transnational/work/,[copyright holder].

b) In one case decided by this court, two contracts had been formed and the debtor immediately stated that he could not fulfil the second contract in the time allowed. The court decided to apply para. 326 BGB by analogy, and held that if the debtor, before performance falls due, states that by reason of unforeseen circumstances he will be unable to perform in time, the creditor must set a time within which the debtor is to declare whether or not he will perform on time and must let the debtor know that if performance is not rendered on time, he will decline to accept it [references].

c) This applies equally to a contract for successive or partial deliveries. Here, too, the creditor can and normally must, by analogy with para. 326 BGB before performance has fallen due, set a period within which the debtor must declare, on pain of the creditor's withdrawal, whether or not he will perform the contract according to its terms. The maxim of Treu und Glauben, as the decision in NJW 1976, 326 = WM 1976, 75 explains, requires no less. A debtor who declares that he will not perform his contractual obligations as they fall due and cannot keep to the delivery dates is admittedly guilty of a positive breach of contract, but even so, para. 326 BGB must be applied by analogy, for if before performance falls due the debtor asserts that he will not perform, and or perform on time, the creditor cannot be expected to wait until performance is due and only then proceed under para. 326 BGB. So, where the debtor has seriously and definitively refused to perform on time, the creditor must have the opportunity to arrange covering contracts, which also serves the interests of the debtor. On the other hand, if the debtor has not definitively refused to perform, the creditor must not take him by surprise by withdrawing or claiming damages without prior notice.

d) Here, then, it was necessary to set a time for performance under para. 326 BGB unless the defendant had already declared, unequivocally and definitively, that it would under no circumstances deliver the four million flowerpots within the contractual period, and any attempt to persuade him otherwise would clearly have been futile.

aa) It is generally agreed that strict tests should be applied before finding that a debtor has made such a declaration, since the purpose of fixing a time for performance is to make him face the dilemma of accepting the consequences of para. 326 BGB or avoiding them by due performance. Thus setting a period for performance can only be dispensed with if the debtor has already unequivocally and definitively made it clear that he does not want, and would not use, any time to perform, if no change in his attitude is to be expected and if notice under para. 326 BGB can be seen to be an empty and futile formality [references}.

bb) The court below misunderstood these requirements. It said that it was unnecessary to set a time here because the defendant had repeatedly said that it was unable to deliver more or more rapidly and had therefore adopted a policy of rationing. It is true that the defendant did say this, but the court made no finding that the defendant had thereby said "its final word" and that any fixing of time would be a futile formality. No such finding could be drawn from the correspondence between the parties.... We cannot therefore exclude the possibility that the defendant would have delivered the agreed quantity of flowerpots in accordance with the contract if the plaintiff had timeously referred to the time for performance set in the contract of September 1967 and had required the defendant, under threat of refusal to accept under para. 326 BGB, to state within a given time whether or not it would perform the contract. The plaintiff did not do this, but accepted short deliveries from the defendant, admittedly under protest; it cannot therefore now claim damages under para. 326 BGB for non-delivery of the balance of the order.

2. Common Law

U.S.A.

Delchi Carrier SpA v. Rotorex Corporation
71 F. 3d 1024, 2nd Cir. 1995

WINTER, Circuit Judge.

[Facts: Rotorex Corporation, a New York corporation, appeals from a judgment of $1,785,722.44 in damages for lost profits and other consequential damages awarded to Delchi, an Italian manufacturer of air conditioners. Delchi cross-appeals from the denial of certain incidental and consequential damages [...]]

[...]After several unsuccessful attempts to cure the defects in the compressors, Delchi asked Rotorex to supply new compressors conforming to the original sample and specifications. Rotorex refused, claiming that the performance specifications were "inadvertently communicated" to Delchi.

[...]Delchi was unable to obtain in a timely fashion substitute compressors from other sources and thus suffered a loss [...] Delchi filed the instant action under the United Nations Convention on Contracts for the International Sale of Goods ("CISG" or "the Convention") for breach of contract and failure to deliver conforming goods.

[...] Judge Munson [...] held Rotorex liable to Delchi for $1,248,331.87. This amount included consequential damages for: (i) lost profits resulting from a diminished sales level [...] (ii) expenses that Delchi incurred in attempting to remedy the nonconformity of the compressors, (iii) the cost of expediting shipment of previously ordered Sanyo compressors after Delchi rejected the Rotorex compressors, and (iv) costs of handling and storing the rejected compressors. The district court also awarded prejudgment interest under CISG art. 78.

The court denied Delchi's claim for damages based on other expenses, including: (i) shipping, customs, and incidentals relating to the two shipments of Rotorex compressors; (ii) the cost of obsolete insulation and tubing [...]; (iii) the cost of obsolete tooling [...]; and (iv) labor costs for four days when Delchi's production line was idle [...] Finally, the court denied recovery on Delchi's claim of 4000 additional lost sales in Italy. [...]

Under the CISG, if the breach is "fundamental" the buyer may either require delivery of substitute goods, CISG art. 46, or declare the contract void, CISG art. 49, and seek damages. With regard to what kind of breach is fundamental, Article 25 provides: [see supra p.146–147]. [...]the district court's conclusion that Rotorex was liable for a fundamental breach of contract under the Convention was proper.

We turn now to the district court's award of damages[...]

The CISG provides:[see supra, CISG Art. 74 p.146] [...]

Because of Rotorex's breach, Delchi had to shut down its manufacturing operation for a few days [...] Delchi lost sales in the spring and early summer. We therefore conclude that the district court's findings regarding lost sales are not clearly erroneous. [...]

The CISG requires that damages be limited by the familiar principle of foreseeability established in *Hadley v. Baxendale,* 156 Eng.Rep. 145 (1854). CISG art. 74. [...]The district court was entitled to rely upon the documents and testimony regarding these lost sales and was well within its authority in deciding which orders were proven with sufficient certainty.[...]

In the absence of a specific provision in the CISG for calculating lost profits, the district court was correct to use the standard formula employed by most American courts and to deduct only variable costs from sales revenue to arrive at a figure for lost profits.[...]

The Convention provides that a contract plaintiff may collect damages to compensate for the full loss.[...]

An award for lost profits will not compensate Delchi for the expenses in question.[...] to award damages for costs actually incurred in no way creates a double recovery and instead furthers the purpose of giving the injured party damages "equal to the loss." CISG art. 74.

The only remaining inquiries, therefore, are whether the expenses were reasonably foreseeable and legitimate incidental or consequential damages. The expenses incurred by Delchi for shipping, customs, and related matters for the two returned shipments of Rotorex compressors, including storage expenses for the second shipment at Genoa, were clearly foreseeable and recoverable incidental expenses. [...] To deny reimbursement to Delchi for these incidental damages would effectively cut into the lost profits award. The same is true of unreimbursed tooling expenses and the cost of the useless insulation and tubing materials. These are legitimate consequential damages that in no way duplicate lost profits damages.[...]

The labor expense incurred as a result of the production line shutdown of May 16–19, 1988 is also a reasonably foreseeable result of delivering nonconforming compressors for installation in air conditioners.

Jacob & Youngs, Inc. v. Kent
230 N.Y. 239, 129 N.E. 889, 1921

CARDOZO, J.

The plaintiff built a country residence for the defendant at a cost of upwards of $77,000, and now sues to recover a balance of $3,483.46, remaining unpaid. The work of construction ceased in June, 1914, and the defendant then began to occupy the dwelling. There was no complaint of defective performance until March, 1915. One of the specifications for the plumbing work provides that——

'All wrought-iron pipe must be well galvanized, lap welded pipe of the grade known as 'standard pipe' of Reading manufacture.'

The defendant learned in March, 1915, that some of the pipe, instead of being made in Reading, was the product of other factories. The plaintiff was accordingly directed by the architect to do the work anew. The plumbing was then encased within the walls except in a few places where it had to be exposed. Obedience to the order meant more than the substitution of other pipe. It meant the demolition at great expense of substantial parts of the completed structure. The plaintiff left the work untouched, and asked for a certificate that the final payment was due. Refusal of the certificate was followed by this suit.

[...]

The courts never say that one who makes a contract fills the measure of his duty by less than full performance. They do say, however, that an omission, both trivial and innocent, will sometimes be atoned for by allowance of the resulting damage, and will not always be the breach of a condition to be followed by a forfeiture.[...]

We must weigh the purpose to be served, the desire to be gratified, the excuse for deviation from the letter, the cruelty of enforced adherence. Then only can we tell whether literal fulfillment is to be implied by law as a condition. This is not to say that the parties are not free by apt and certain words to effectuate a purpose that performance of every term shall be a condition of recovery. That question is not here. This is merely to say that the law will be slow to impute the purpose, in the silence of the parties, where the significance of the default is grievously out of proportion to the oppression of the forfeiture.[...]

In the circumstances of this case, we think the measure of the allowance is not the cost of replacement, which would be great, but the difference in value, which would be either nominal or nothing.[...] The owner is entitled to the money which will permit him to complete, unless the cost of completion is grossly and unfairly out of proportion to the good to be attained. When that is true, the measure is the difference in value.[...] The rule that gives a remedy in cases of substantial performance with compensation for defects of trivial or inappreciable importance has been developed by the courts as an instrument of justice. The measure of the allowance must be shaped to the same end.[...]

MCLAUGHLIN, J.

I dissent. The plaintiff did not perform its contract. Its failure to do so was either intentional or due to gross neglect which, under the uncontradicted facts, amounted to the same thing, nor did it make any proof of the cost of compliance, where compliance was possible.[...]

The defendant had a right to contract for what he wanted. He had a right before making payment to get what the contract called for. It is no answer to this suggestion to say that the pipe put in was just as good as that made by the Reading Manufacturing Company, or that the difference in value between such pipe and the pipe made by the Reading Manufacturing Company would be either 'nominal or nothing.' Defendant contracted for pipe made by the Reading Manufacturing Company. What his reason was for requiring this kind of pipe is of no importance. He wanted that and was entitled to it. It may have been a mere whim on his part, but even so, he had a right to this kind of pipe, regardless of whether some other kind, according to the opinion of the contractor or experts, would have been 'just as good, better, or done just as well.'[...]The rule, therefore, of substantial performance, with damages for unsubstantial omissions, has no application. [...]

HISCOCK, C. J., and HOGAN and CRANE, JJ., concur with CARDOZO, J. POUND and ANDREWS, JJ., concur with MCLAUGHLIN, J.

U.K.

Hadley and Another v. Baxendale and Others
CLVI ER 145, 9 EX. 341, 1854

[Facts: Where the plaintiffs, the owners of a flour mill, sent a broken iron shaft to an office of the defendants, who were common carriers, to be conveyed by them, and the defendants' clerk, who attended at the office, was told that the mill was stopped, that the shaft must be delivered immediately, and that a special entry, if necessary, must be made to hasten its delivery; and the delivery of the broken shaft to the consignee, to whom it had been sent by the plaintiffs as a pattern, by which to make a new shaft, was delayed for an unreasonable time; in consequence of which, the plaintiffs did not receive the new shaft for some days after the time they ought to have received it, and they were consequently unable to work their mill from want of the new shaft, and thereby incurred a loss of profits.]

The judgment of the Court was now delivered by ALDERSON, B.

[...]

Now we think the proper rule is such as the present is this: Where two parties have made a contract which one of them has broken, the damages which the other party ought to receive in respect of such breach of contract should be such as may fairly and reasonably be considered either arising naturally, i.e., according to the usual course of things, from such breach of contract itself, or such as may reasonably be supposed to have been in the contemplation of both parties, at the time they made the contract, as the probable result of the breach of it. Now, if the special circumstances under which the contract was actually made where communicated by the plaintiffs to the defendants, and thus known to both parties, the damages resulting from the breach of such a contract, which they would reasonably contemplate, would be the amount of injury which would ordinarily follow from a breach of contract under these special circumstances so known and communicated. But, on the other hand, if these special circumstances were wholly unknown to the party breaking the contract, he, at the most, could only be supposed to have had in his contemplation the amount of injury which would arise generally, and in the great multitude of cases not affected by any special circumstances, from such a breach of contract. For, had the special circumstances been known, the parties might have specially provided for the breach of contract by special terms as to the damages in that case; and of this advantage it would be very unjust to deprive them.[...] Now, in the present case, if we are to apply the principles above laid down, we find that the only circumstances here communicated by the plaintiffs to the defendants at the time the contract was made, were, that the article to be carried was the broken shaft of a mill, and that the plaintiffs were the millers of that mill. But how do these circumstances shew reasonably that the profits of the mill must be stopped by an unreasonable delay in the delivery of the broken shaft by the carrier to the third person? Suppose the plaintiffs had another shaft in their possession put up or putting up at the time,[...]Or, again, suppose that, at the time of the delivery to the carrier, the machinery of the mill had been in other respects defective, [...] in the great multitude of cases of millers sending off broken shafts to third persons by a carrier under ordinary circumstances, such consequences would not, in all probability, have occurred; and these special circumstances were here never communicated by the plaintiffs to the defendants. It follows, therefore, that the loss of profits here cannot reasonably be considered such a consequence of the breach of contract as could have been fairly and reasonably contemplated by both the parties when they made this contract. [...] The Judge ought, therefore, to have told the jury, that, upon the facts then before them, they ought not to take the loss of profits into consideration at all in estimating the damages.[...]

Ruxley Electronics Ltd. Forsyth (H.L. (E))
[1996] A.C. 344

LORD BRIDGE OF HARWICH. My Lords, damages for breach of contract must reflect, as accurately as the circumstances allow, the loss which the claimant has sustained because he did not get what he bargained for. There is no question of punishing the contract breaker.[...]

The circumstances giving rise to the present appeal exemplify a situation which one might suppose to be of not infrequent occurrence. A landowner contracts for building works to be executed on his land. When the work is complete it serves the practical purpose for which it was required perfectly satisfactorily. But in some minor respect the finished work falls short of the contract specification. The difference in commercial value between the work as built and the work as specified is nil. But the owner can honestly say:

"This work does not please me as well as would that for which I expressly stipulated. It does not satisfy my personal preference. In terms of amenity, convenience or aesthetic satisfaction I have lost something." Nevertheless the contractual defect could only be remedied by demolishing the work and starting again from scratch. The cost of doing this would be so great in proportion to any benefit it would confer on the owner that no reasonable owner would think of incurring it. What is the measure of the loss which the owner has sustained in these circumstances?[...]

LORD JAUNCEY OF TULLICHETTLE. My Lords, the respondent entered into a contract with the appellants for the construction by them of a swimming pool at his house in Kent. The contract provided for the pool having a maximum depth of 7 feet 6 inches but, as built, its maximum depth was only 6 feet. The respondents sought to recover as damages for breach of contract the cost of demolition of the existing pool and construction of a new one of the required depth. The trial judge made the following findings which are relevant to this appeal: (1) the pool as constructed was perfectly safe to dive into; (2) there was no evidence that the shortfall in depth had decreased the value of the pool; (3) the only practicable method of achieving a pool of the required depth would be to demolish the existing pool and reconstruct a new one at a cost of £21,560; (4) he was not satisfied that the respondent intended to build a new pool at such a cost; (5) in addition such cost would be wholly disproportionate to the disadvantage of having a pool of a depth of only 6 feet as opposed to 7 feet 6 inches and it would therefore be unreasonable to carry out the works; and (6) that the respondent was entitled to damages for loss of amenity in the sum of £2,500.

The Court of Appeal by a majority (Staughton and Mann L.J., Dillon L.J. dissenting) allowed the appeal holding that the only way in which the respondent could achieve his contractual objective was by reconstructing the pool at a cost of £21,560 which was accordingly a reasonable venture. [...]

Damages are designed to compensate for an established loss and not to provide a gratuitous benefit to the aggrieved party from which it follows that the reasonableness of an award of damages is to be linked directly to the loss sustained. If it is unreasonable in a particular case to award the cost of reinstatement it must be because the loss sustained does not extend to the need to reinstate. A failure to achieve the precise contractual objective does not necessarily result in the loss which is occasioned by a total failure. This was recognised by the High Court of Australia [...]

It was submitted that where the objective of a building contract involved satisfaction of a personal preference the only measure of damages available for a breach involving failure to achieve such satisfaction was the cost of reinstatement. In my view this is not the case. Personal preference may well be a factor in reasonableness and hence in determining what loss has been suffered but it cannot per se be determinative of what that loss is.

My Lords, the trial judge found that it would be unreasonable to incur the cost of demolishing the existing pool and building a new and deeper one. In so doing he implicitly recognised that the respondent's loss did not extend to the cost of reinstatement. He was, in my view, entirely justified in reaching that conclusion. It therefore follows that the appeal must be allowed. [...]

LORD MUSTILL.

[...]It is a common feature of small building works performed on residential property that the cost of the work is not fully reflected by an increase in the market value of the house, and that comparatively minor deviations from specification or sound workmanship may have no direct financial effect at all. Yet the householder must surely be entitled to say that he chose to obtain from the builder a promise to produce a particular result because he wanted to make his house more comfortable, more convenient and more conformable to his own particular tastes; not because he had in mind that the work might increase the amount which he would receive if, contrary to expectation, he thought it expedient in the future to exchange his home for cash. To say that in order to escape unscathed the builder has only to show that to the mind of the average onlooker, or the average potential buyer, the results which he has produced seem just as good as those which he had promised would make a part of the promise illusory, and unbalance the bargain. [...] The court should honour that choice. Pacta sunt servanda. If the appellant's argument leads to the conclusion that in all cases like the present the employer is entitled to no more than nominal damages, the average householder would say that there must be something wrong with the law.[...]

There are not two alternative measures of damage, at opposite poles, but only one; namely, the loss truly suffered by the promisee. In some cases the loss cannot be fairly measured except by reference to the full cost of repairing the deficiency in performance. In others, and in particular those where the contract is designed to fulfil a purely commercial purpose, the loss will very often consist only of the monetary detriment brought about by the breach of contract. But these remedies are not exhaustive, for the law must cater for those occasions where the value of the promise to the promisee exceeds the financial enhancement of his position which full performance will secure. This excess, often referred to in the literature as the "consumer surplus"

[...] is usually incapable of precise valuation in terms of money, exactly because it represents a personal, subjective and non-monetary gain. Nevertheless where it exists the law should recognise it and compensate the promisee if the misperformance takes it away.[...]

LORD LLOYD OF BEWICK.

Reasonableness

The starting point is *Robinson v. Harman*, 1 Exch. 850, where Parke B. said, at p.855:

> "The rule of the common law is, that where a party sustains a loss by reason of a breach of contract, he is, so far as money can do it, to be placed in the same situation, with respect to damages, as if the contract had been performed."

This does not mean that in every case of breach of contract the plaintiff can obtain the monetary equivalent of specific performance. It is first necessary to ascertain the loss the plaintiff has in fact suffered by reason of the breach. If he has suffered no loss, as sometimes happens, he can recover no more than nominal damages. For the object of damages is always to compensate the plaintiff, not to punish the defendant. [...]I am far from saying that personal preferences are irrelevant when choosing the appropriate measure of damages[...] But such cases should not be elevated into a separate category with special rules. If, to take an example mentioned in the course of argument, a landowner wishes to build a folly in his grounds, it is no answer to a claim for defective workmanship that many people might regard the presence of a well built folly as reducing the value of the estate. The eccentric landowner is entitled to his whim, provided the cost of reinstatement is not unreasonable. But the difficulty of that line of argument in the present case is that the judge, as is clear from his judgment, took Mr. Forsyth's personal preferences and predilections into account. Nevertheless, he found as a fact that the cost of reinstatement was unreasonable in the circumstances. The Court of Appeal ought not to have disturbed that finding. [...]

Chapter Eight

Justifiable/Justified Non-Performance

As briefly illustrated above, parties enter into long-term contractual relationships at a certain point in time with the expectation that, at a later point in time, each will receive from the other the performance planned for in exchange for the performance that each one is committed to carry out for the benefit of the other. Parties direct their attention towards a certain contract and commit their resources to an exchange of agreed upon performances rather than enter into a contract with someone else and commit their resources towards other, identical or different, performances. However, between the time the contract is negotiated and entered into on the basis of the circumstances that exist at that time and the time specified for the performances to be carried out, many different, unexpected or unforeseen events may occur in such a manner as to upset and disrupt the parties' plans as laid down in the contract. Some of these events may occur, in totality or in part only, because of the fault or the negligence on the part of one party or the other. We do not intend to consider this situation here, for reasons of space limitation and because the previous Section on Performance and Damages and the Section on Good Faith may offer sufficient insight into the acceptable solutions to the problems raised the negligent interference of one party or the other in the performance of the obligations created by the contract. Our interest will be directed here at those events or changes in circumstances which occur outside and beyond the will or actions of the parties. These events may fit under a variety of adjectives: 'political,' 'economic,' 'financial,' 'natural.' Yet, they all have in common the fact that they may serve as a justification for a party not to perform her side of the bargain, or carry out a modified and adjusted performance of the original obligation. For our purpose, all these events will be lumped under a series of 'legal' labels which, if each one was taken separately as is done elsewhere, could otherwise be given slightly different legal treatments. The legal labels we will refer to are the following: Frustration, Imprévision, Force Majeure, Hardship, Impossibility ... After having read all the sources of law presented hereunder, the reader will be in a position to draw the appropriate distinctions between the civil law and the common law in their use or not of these different means of justifying the non-performance of an obligation.

A. Civil Law

1. Roman Law

S.P. Scott, A.M., The Civil Law including....
The Enactments of Justinian...
Vol. IX, 1932

The Digest or Pandects — Book XLV

15. The Same, On Sabinus, Book XXVII

Hence doubt arises, if a portion of the house having been built it should afterwards be destroyed by fire, whether the entire time for rebuilding it should be computed, or whether only the remaining time should be taken into consideration. The better opinion is that the entire time for rebuilding it should be granted.

33. Pomponius, On Sabinus, Book XXV

If Stichus is promised to be delivered on a certain day, and dies before that day arrives, the promisor will not be liable.

35. Paulus, On Sabinus, Book XII

If I stipulate for an act to be performed which Nature does not permit to take place, the obligation does not become operative, any more than when I stipulate something shall be given which is not possible, unless it is the fault of someone that this cannot be done.

37. Paulus, On Sabinus, Book XII

If I stipulate for a certain sum of money, for instance, what is in a chest, and it is lost without the fault of the promisor, nothing will be due to us.

The Digest or Pandects — Book L

185. The Same (Celsus), Digest, Book VIII

No obligation is binding which is impossible.

2. Contemporary Civil Law

La. Civ. C.

Art. 1873: An obligor is not liable for his failure to perform when it is caused by a fortuitous event that makes performance impossible.

An obligor is, however, liable for his failure to perform when he has assumed the risk of such a fortuitous event.

An obligor is liable also when the fortuitous event occurred after he has been put in default.

An obligor is likewise liable when the fortuitous event that caused his failure to perform has been preceded by his fault, without which the failure would not have occurred.

Art. 1874: An obligor who had been put in default when a fortuitous event made his performance impossible is not liable for his failure to perform if the fortuitous event would have likewise destroyed the object of the performance in the hands of the obligee had performance been timely rendered.

That obligor is, however, liable for the damage caused by his delay.

Art. 1875: A fortuitous event is one that, at the time the contract was made, could not have been reasonably foreseen.

Art. 1876: When the entire performance owed by one party has become impossible because of a fortuitous event, the contract is dissolved.

The other party may then recover any performance he has already rendered.

Art. 1877: When a fortuitous event has made a party's performance impossible in part, the court may reduce the other party's counterperformance proportionally, or, according to the circumstances, may declare the contract dissolved.

Fr. Civ. C.

Art. 1134. [see supra p.129]

Art. 1137(1): An obligation to preserve the thing, whether the contract has for its object the benefit of one party only, or whether it has for its object the common interest of the parties, imposes on the party in charge of preserving the thing the duty to act as a prudent administrator (bon père de famille).

Art. 1147: Should it be the case, an obligor is liable to pay damages either on account of his failure to perform, or on account of his delay in performing, whenever he is unable to prove that the non-performance was caused by a fortuitous event for which he cannot be held liable, or that he did not act in bad faith.

Art. 1148: No damages are owed when, because of force majeure or a fortuitous event, an obligor was prevented from giving or doing what he was bound to give or do, or when he did what he was forbidden from doing.

Art. 1302: When a certain and identified thing which was the object of an obligation, has perished, is out of commerce, or is lost in such a manner that one absolutely cannot know of its existence, the obligation is extinguished is the thing has perished or has been lost without the obligor's fault and before he had been put in default ... The obligor must prove the fortuitous event he alleges.

BGB

Section 242. [see supra p.130]

Section 275. Exclusion of the duty of performance.

(1) A claim for performance cannot be made in so far as it is impossible for the obligor or for anyone else to perform.

(2) The obligor may refuse to perform in so far as performance requires expenditure which, having regard to the subject matter of the obligation and the principle of good faith, is manifestly disproportionate to the obligee's interest in performance. When determining what may reasonably be required of the obligor, regard must also be had to whether he is responsible for the impediment to performance.

(3) Moreover, the obligor may refuse to perform, if he is to effect the performance in in person and, after weighing up the obligee's interest in performance and the impediment to performance, performance cannot be reasonably required of the obligor.

Section 276. Responsibility of the obligor

(1) The obligor is liable for deliberate and negligent acts or omissions, unless the existence of a stricter or more lenient degree of liability is specified or to be inferred from the other subject matter of the obligation, ...

(2) A person acts negligently if he fails to observe the relevant accepted standards of care ...

Section 313. Interference with the basis of the transaction

(1) If circumstances upon which a contract was based have materially changed after the conclusion of the contract and if the parties would not have concluded the contract or would have done so upon different terms if they had foreseen that change, adaptation of the contract may be claimed in so far as, having regard to all the circumstances of the specific case, in particular the contractual or statutory allocation of risk, it cannot reasonably be expected that a party should continue to be bound by the contract in its unaltered form.

(2) If material assumptions that have become the basis of the contract subsequently turn out to be incorrect, they are treated in the same way as a change in circumstances.

(3) If adaptation of the contract is not possible or cannot reasonably be expected of one party, the disadvantaged party may withdraw from the contract. In the case of recurring obligations, the right to terminate takes the place of the right to withdraw.

Section 323. Withdrawal for non-performance or for performance not in accordance with the contract

(6) Withdrawal is excluded, if the obligee is solely or overwhelmingly responsible for the circumstances which would entitle him to withdraw from the contract or if a circumstance for which the obligor is not responsible materializes at a time when the obligee is in default through non-acceptance.

C.C.Q.

Art. 1590. [see supra p.131]

Art. 1582: A creditor who is in default bears the reasonable costs of preservation of the thing, as well as any costs that may be incurred for the sale of the thing and the deposit of the proceeds.

He also bears the risks of loss of the thing by superior force.

Art. 1693: A debtor is released where he cannot perform an obligation by reason of a superior force and before he is in default, or where, although he was in default, the creditor could not, in any case, benefit by the performance of the obligation by reason of that superior force, unless, in either case, the debtor has expressly assumed the risk of superior force.

The burden of proof of superior force is on the debtor.

Art. 1694: A debtor released by impossibility of performance may not exact performance of the correlative obligation of the creditor; if the performance has already been rendered, restitution is owed.

Where the debtor has performed part of his obligation, the creditor remains bound to perform his own obligation to the extent of his enrichment.

It. Civ. C.[32]

1218. Liability of debtor. The debtor who does not exactly render due performance is liable for damages (1223) unless he proves that the non-performance or delay was due to impossibility of performance for a cause not imputable to him (1256 ff.)

1256. Definitive impossibility and temporary impossibility. An obligation is extinguished when its performance becomes impossible for a cause not imputable to the debtor (1218).

If the impossibility is only temporary the debtor is not liable for delay in performance as long as it continues to exist. However, the obligation is extinguished if the impossibility continues until, depending on the source of the obligation or the nature of its subject matter, the debtor can no longer be held bound to perform the obligation or the creditor is no longer interested in the performance (1174).

1257. Loss of specified thing. A performance that has as its subject matter a specified thing is also considered to be impossible when such thing is lost without it being possible to prove its destruction.

In case the thing is subsequently found, the provisions of the second paragraph of the preceding article apply.

1463. Total impossibility. In contracts providing for mutual counter-performance, the party released for supervening impossibility of the performance due(1256) cannot demand performance by the other party, and he is bound to restore that which he has already received, in accordance with the rules concerning restitution of payments not due (2033 f).

1464. Partial impossibility. When the performance of one party has become impossible only in part (1258), the other party has a right to a corresponding reduction of the performance due by him, and he can also withdraw from the contract if he lacks an appreciable interest in partial performance (1181).

---

32. Translated by M. Beltramo, G. Longo, J.H. Merryman, 1969.

1467. Contract for mutual counterperformances. In contracts for continuous or periodic performance or for deferred performance, if extraordinary and unforeseeable events make the performance of one of the parties excessively onerous, the party who owes such performance can demand dissolution of the contract, with the effects set forth in article 1458.

Dissolution cannot be demanded if the supervening onerousness is part of the normal risk of the contract.

A party against whom dissolution is demanded can avoid it by offering to modify equitably the conditions of the contract.

1468. Contracts with obligations of one party only. In the case contemplated in the preceding article, if the contract is one in which only one of the parties has assumed obligations, he can demand a reduction in his performance or a modification of the manner of performance, sufficient to restore it to an equitable basis.

Marcel Planiol, Georges Ripert, Traité Pratique de Droit Civil Français
LGDJ, 1954, vol VII Obligations.[33]

Section II. — Impossibility of performance.

1314. Variety of effects. — An impossibility to perform an obligation carries with it many consequences. If the impossibility exists as of the time of formation of the contract, it prevents its formation; it is nul because of a lack of object. If it appears later, without any fault on the part of the obligor, it prevents the obligation from surviving: to the impossible no one can be held. The obligor is not only released from the duty to carry out the performance he promised, but he is also exonerated from the duty to pay damages in lieu of a specific performance which has become impossible.... An impossibility to perform can be considered as a ground for extinguishing obligations only to the extent that it is the cause of the disappearance of the very obligation of the obligor.

1316. Conditions which must be met by an impossibility to perform. — An obligation is extinguished only if the impossibility occurs after the obligation was created; otherwise the obligation would not have come into exis-

---

33. Author's liberal translation.

tence. But, in addition, the impossibility must exist at the time the performance is due and definitive ... Existence of an obligation and the possibility of its performance are two different things. An impossibility which occurs before the performance is due but which does not look like it will be permanent has no effect, then, on the existence of the obligation.... The impossibility cannot be due to the fault of the obligor.... [If due to the fault of the obligor] he will not be exonerated ... and he will have to perform an 'equivalent' obligation ... under the form of damages ...

1317. Impossibility without fault.—.... The impossibility must be absolute and have been caused independently from the obligor's will, so much so that the obligor could not have anticipated it nor resisted it. In other words, the impossibility must meet the characteristics of force majeure. [see Fr. Civ. C. articles 1147 and 1148 supra p.167–168]

Ph. Malaurie, L. Aynès, Ph. Stoffel-Munck
Droit Civil, Les Obligations, Defrénois 2003[34]

§3. Grounds for exoneration

[...] An obligor cannot be held liable when the non-performance of his obligation can be imputed to a 'foreign cause' (fortuitous event), unless the obligor was held to an obligation of warranty. The most typical is force majeure, to which are assimilated the 'fact' of the obligee and the fact of a third person. These 'causes' (grounds) exonerate the obligor, unless they have only a temporary effect, in which case they merely suspend the contract.

I–Force majeure

952. Reasonable.— [...].Just as the English theory of *frustration* is now used in reference to the notion of a 'reasonable person,' in France force majeure tends to be defined by an event which is reasonably irresistible, unforeseeable and exterior which, most often requires a case by case appraisal.

953. Irresistible.—The event must be irresistible; it is the main requirement; if it could have been overcome, even though the performance would have been more difficult and onerous, the obligor would still be held liable for not

---

34. Author's liberal translation.

having performed; there does not exist any financial force majeure.... [...] The difficult question is to determine at which point in time there is 'irresistibility.' It is obvious that law is not absolute and cannot expect the obligor to be a 'superman,' Tarzan ... Rambo ... All is necessarily relative. The real question to ask is the following: should irresistibility be evaluated *in abstracto* or *in concreto*? There are cases on both sides....

955. Unforeseeable.— ... the event ... must have been unforeseeable at the time of perfection of the contract. If the obligor could have foreseen the event, he will be at fault for non having taken the necessary measures.... (same comment with respect to "absolute" unforeseeability as for "irresistibility" above); as with respect to irrestibility, unforeseeability depends on the circumstances ...

956. Exterior.— The event must be 'exterior' to the obligor, otherwise he should be liable. Exteriority is implied by the expression of " a cause (source) foreign to the obligor" so that the event cannot be imputed to the obligor....

II.–Fact of the creditor, of a third person or of the prince

958. Fact of the creditor.— The fact of the creditor(the victim) exonerates the obligor. This is a rational view: if the damage was caused by the victim, it cannot be held against the obligor....

959. Fact of a third person or the prince.— (there is there also a ground for not holding the obligor liable) if the fact was irresistible, unforeseeable and if the obligor was not to be held liable in one way or another. It is a type of force majeure....

B. Common Law

1. Common Law in the U.K.

William Blackstone, Commentaries on the Laws of England
by G.Chase, 1890

Chapter XXII. *Of Proceedings in the Courts of Equity.*

3. With respect to the mode of *relief.* [...] A court of equity will compel them [executory agreements] to be carried into strict execution, unless where

it is improper or impossible; instead of giving damages for their non-performance ...

P.S. Atiyah

(opus cited)

[...] A key area of the law was the doctrine of frustration, which,..., enables a court to declare that a contract is at an end when it becomes impossible to perform it without fault on the part of either party. [...] The seminal case was the decision of the House of Lords in *Davis Contractors v. Fareham UDC* and the following passage from the speech of Lord Radcliffe in this case explains how it was possible to move from one theory to the other:

Lord Loreburn ascribes the dissolution to an implied term of the contract that was actually made. This approach is in line with the tendency of English Courts to refer all the consequences of a contract to the will of those who made it. But there is something of logical difficulty in seeing how the parties could even impliedly have provided for something which, *ex hypothesi,* they neither expected nor foresaw; ... The legal effect of frustration does not 'depend on their (the individuals concerned) intention or their opinion, or even knowledge as to the event.' On the contrary, it seems that, when the event occurs, 'the meaning of the contract must be taken to be, not what the parties did intend (for they had neither thought nor intention regarding it), but that which the parties, as fair and reasonable men, would presumably have agreed upon if, having such possibilities in view, they had made express provision as to their several rights and liabilities in the event of its occurrence.'

[...] There are two main classes of cases in question here. Where the entire performance of the contract proves substantially impossible, either because of pre-existing facts or because of unforeseen and unforeseeable developments occurring without anybody's fault, the courts have been loath to hold a contracting party liable, especially in the latter case. In other words, the law does not usually treat a person who has contracted to do something as having taken the risk that the whole performance may prove utterly impossible, either initially or owing to later events. [...]

Where the entire performance of a contract becomes substantially impossible without any fault on either side, the contract is prima facie dissolved by the doctrine of frustration. For instance, where a person contracted to let a hall to the plaintiff for use for some concerts, and the hall was accidentally destroyed by fire before the date of the first concert, it was held that the contract was dissolved. So also a contract for personal service will normally be dissolved by the death or prolonged illness or ... the imprisonment of the employee....

The position is slightly more difficulty where the contract is one of long duration and the performance is merely interrupted and not actually prevented *in toto.* In these cases the contract is prima facie dissolved if the interruption is likely to prove so lengthy that to compel the parties to resume the contract later would, in effect, be to compel them to enter into a new contract. [...] On the other hand, where the interruption, even on the most pessimistic view, is unlikely to affect more than a small fraction of the contract, it is not frustrated. [...]

G.H. Treitel
(opus cited)

Chapter 20 Frustration

(7) Impossibility and impracticability

(a) IMPRACTICABILITY DISTINGUISHED FROM IMPOSSIBILITY. The doctrine of frustration originated in cases where performance was said to have become "impossible." That, in itself, is something of a relative term. What is "impossible" depends partly on the current state of technology, and partly on the amount of trouble and expense to which one is prepared to go to achieve it.[...] For this reason the current trend in the United States is to abandon the very words "impossible" and "impossibility" and to use instead the terms "impracticable" and "impracticability" ...

(b) IMPRACTICABILITY GENERALLY NO EXCUSE. [...] it appears that "impracticability" is not generally sufficient to frustrate a contract in English law ... Lord Radcliffe said : " It is not hardship or inconvenience or material loss itself which calls the principle of frustration into play. There must be as well a change in the significance of the obligation that the thing undertaken would, if performed, be a different thing from that contracted for ... Where performance would, in view of changed circumstances, cause not merely extra expense but acute personal hardship to one party, it has been said that "equitable relief may ... be refused because of an unforeseen change of circumstances not amounting to legal frustration." But in such cases the contract is not discharged: the defendant remains liable in damages even though specific performance is refused on the ground of severe hardship. [...]

2. Frustration of Purpose

Frustration of purpose is, in a sense, the converse of impracticability. The two ideas resemble each other in that neither is concerned with cases in which performance has become impossible. Impracticability is said to arise when a *supplier* of goods, services or other facilities alleges that performance of his own promise has become so burdensome to him that he should no longer be bound to render it. The argument of frustration of purpose, on the other hand, is put forward by the recipient of the goods, services or facilities: it is that supervening events have so greatly reduced the value to him of the other party's performance that he should no longer be bound to accept and to pay the agreed price ...

The more recent authorities show that "the frustrated expectations and intentions of one party to a contract do not necessarily, or indeed usually, lead to the frustration of that contract." They make it difficult to establish the defence of frustration of purpose; but they do not make it impossible ...

Butterworths

(opus cited)

E. Termination by Frustration

General

Concept

7.49 The modern concept of frustration was stated in the following terms by Lord Radcliffe in *Davis Contractors Ltd v Fareham UDC:*

> [F]rustration occurs whenever the law recognizes that without default of either party a contractual obligation has become incapable of being performed because the circumstances in which performance is called for would render it a thing radically different from that which was undertaken by the contract. *Non haec in foedera veni.* It was not this that I promised to do.

[...] the mere fact that an event deprives a party to a contract of benefits which were expected from its performance, or even renders performance physically impossible, does not imply that the doctrine of frustration can be used as an excuse for not performing, since a party may be found to have taken the risk of such an eventuality, or undertaken an absolute promise to perform ...

Scope of the doctrine

7.51 The doctrine of frustration is a flexible doctrine which has been applied in a wide variety of contexts and to virtually all types of contracts, including construction contracts; ... employment contracts; contracts for the sale of goods; ... It may be confidently stated that there is no class of contract which falls outside the scope of the doctrine.

Application of the doctrine

7.52 The general rule is that the impact of an event relied on as a frustrating event must be assessed at the time of its occurrence. An event relied upon as frustrating the contract is 'something which happens in the world of fact.'.. Because of the factual element, the relevant conclusion of law will, in many cases, be 'almost completely determined by what the judge or arbitrator determines as the commercial significance of the event relied upon as frustrating the contract ...

Basis for the doctrine

7.53 The acceptance of Lord Radcliffe's formulation of the concept of frustration implies that the doctrine is primarily based on construction of the contract. The court can only decide what a party promised to do by construing the contract and the modern cases emphasise construction as the most satisfactory basis for the doctrine ...

Proof of frustration

Impossibility

7.55 Most cases of frustration involve an element of impossibility. It is therefore hardly surprising that the doctrine of frustration first emerged in cases where specific subject matter had been destroyed (or perished) without the fault of either party.... Where the performance of a contract has a personal element, death or incapacity may frustrate its performance. For example, the death of an employee frustrates a contract of employment.

7.57 Frustration of purpose [...]care must be taken not to treat every change in circumstances as frustration, even if the expectation of one of the parties is to some extent 'frustrated' by an extraneous event. Events frequently occur which cause the expectations of contracting parties to be disappointed, but disappointment is not synonymous with frustration. Thus, the purpose of a contract is not frustrated merely because the benefits which a party expected to obtain from its performance are not realized in full.

The mere fact that an event which was not contemplated by the parties when they entered into the contract has occurred does not amount to frustration. It is the purpose of the contract which must be frustrated. Accordingly, the facts must involve the 'cessation or non-existence of an express condition or state of things going to the root of the contract, and essential to its performance.'

Foresight and terms dealing with frustration

7.61 Although not reproduced in Lord Radcliffe's statement of the concept of frustration in *Davis Contractors Ltd v. Fareham UDC*, it is usually said that the event relied upon as frustrating the contract must not have been foreseen by the parties ... If the event was foreseen, and the contract contains no provision covering the event, the inference may be drawn that the parties agreed to bear the risk of the occurrence of the event. The contract will then not be frustrated. The extent of foresight required has not been the subject of detailed discussion in the authorities ...

Consequences of frustration

Discharge of parties

7.65 When frustration occurs termination is automatic. Moreover, frustration does not merely suspend the parties' obligations, it discharges the parties from the obligation to perform (or to be ready and willing to perform) their contractual duties ...

2. Common Law in the U.S.A.

Restatement, 2d

§ 261. Discharge by Supervening Impracticability

Where, after a contract is made, a party's performance is made impracticable without his fault by the occurrence of an event the non-occurrence of which was a basic assumption on which the contract was made, his duty to render that performance is discharged, unless the language or the circumstances indicate the contrary.

Comment:

a.   Scope. [...] This Section states the general principle under which a party's duty may be so discharged. The following three sections deal with the three categories of cases where this general principle has traditionally been applied: supervening death or incapacity of a person necessary for performance (§ 262), supervening destruction of a specific thing necessary for performance (§ 263}, and supervening prohibition or prevention by law (§ 264}.

§ 265. Discharge by Supervening Frustration

(1) Where, after a contract is made, a party's performance under it is impracticable without his fault because of a fact of which he has no reason to know and the non-existence of which is a basic assumption on which the contract is made, no duty to render that performance arises, unless the language or circumstances indicate the contrary.

(2) Where, at the time a contract is made, a party's principle purpose is substantially frustrated without his fault by a fact of which he has no reason to know and the non-existence of which is a basic assumption on which the contract is made, no duty of that party to render performance arises, unless the language or circumstances indicate the contrary.

UCC

§ 2-613. Casualty to Identified Goods.

Where the contract requires for its performance goods identified when the contract is made, and the goods suffer casualty without fault of either party before the risk of loss passes to the buyer, or in a proper case under a "no arrival, no sale" term (Section 2-324) then

(a) if the loss is total the contract is avoided; and

(b) if the loss is partial or the goods have so deteriorated as no longer to conform to the contract the buyer may nevertheless demand inspection and at his option either treat the contract as avoided or accept the goods with due allowance from the contract price for the deterioration or the deficiency in quantity but without further right against the seller.

§ 2-614. Substituted Performance.

(1) If without fault of either party the agreed berthing, loading, or unloading facilities fail or an agreed type of carrier becomes unavailable or the agreed manner of performance otherwise becomes commercially impracticable but a commercially reasonable substitute is available, the substitute performance must be tendered and accepted.

(2) If the agreed means or manner of payment fails because of domestic or foreign governmental regulation, the seller may withhold or stop delivery

unless the buyer provides a means or manner of payment which is commercially a substantial equivalent. If delivery has already been taken, payment by the means or in the manner provided by the regulation discharges the buyer's obligation unless the regulation is discriminatory, oppressive or predatory.

§ 2-615. Excuse by Failure of Presupposed Conditions.

Except to the extent that a seller may have assumed a greater obligation and subject to section 2-614:

> (a) Delay in performance or nonperformance in whole or in part by a seller that complies with paragraphs (b) and (c) is not a breach of the seller's duty under a contract for sale if performance as agreed has been made impracticable by the occurrence of a contingency the nonoccurrence of which was a basic assumption on which the contract was made or by compliance in good faith with any applicable foreign or domestic governmental regulation or order whether or not it later proves to be invalid.

Official Comment

3. The first test for excuse under this Article in terms of basic assumption is a familiar one. The additional test of commercial impracticability (as contrasted with "impossibility," "frustration of performance" or "frustration of the venture") has been adopted in order to call attention to the commercial character of the criterion chosen by this Article.

4. Increased cost alone does not excuse performance unless the rise in cost is due to some unforeseen contingency which alters the essential nature of the performance. Neither is a rise or a collapse in the market in itself a justification, for that is exactly the type of business risk which business contracts made at fixed prices are intended to cover. But a severe shortage of raw materials or of supplies due to a contingency such as war, embargo, local crop failure, unforeseen shutdown of major sources of supply or the like, which either causes a marked increase in cost or altogether prevents the seller from securing supplies necessary to his performance is within the contemplation of this section.

E. Allan Farnsworth

(opus cited)

Chapter 9 Failure of a Basic Assumption: Mistake, Impracticability and Frustration

§9.1. **Nature of the Problem.** [...] Conventional treatments of the law of contracts have conceptualized the question of excuse under two distinct headings: mistake, which deals with assumptions concerning facts that exist at the time the contract is made; and impracticability and frustration, which deal largely with assumptions concerning circumstances that are expected to exist, including events that are expected to occur, after the contract is made. This conceptual division reflects a sense that the allocation of the risk of error in an assumption should depend on whether the assumption concerns the state of affairs at the time of agreement or at some later time.[...]

C. IMPRACTICABILITY AND FRUSTRATION

§9.5. **Growth of Impossibility as an Excuse.** The common law was slow to give effect to the maxim *impossibilium nulla obligatio est* ("there is no obligation to do the impossible"). Courts were less receptive to claims of excuse based on events occurring after the making of the contract than they were to claims of excuse based on facts that existed at the time of the agreement. [...]

§9.6. **A New Synthesis: The Doctrine of Impracticability.** The common law development ... is synthesized in UCC 2-615, Excuse by Failure of Presupposed Conditions. [...]

Under the new synthesis, the party that claims that a supervening event or "contingency" prevented performance must meet four requirements. First, the event must have made "performance as agreed ... impracticable." Second, the nonoccurrence of the event must have been "a basic assumption on which the contract was made." Third, the impracticability must have resulted without the fault of the party seeking to be excused. Fourth, that party must not have assumed a greater obligation than the law imposes. Although these requirements involve questions of fact, courts have sometimes been reluctant to entrust the granting of excuse on this ground to a jury.[...]

§9.7. **Frustration of Purpose.** The fountainhead of the doctrine of frustration of purpose is the English case of *Krell v. Henry.*

The doctrine announced in *Krell v. Henry* has come to be known as that of frustration of purpose. Cancellation of the procession did not make performance by either party impracticable; it did not prevent Krell from letting Henry use his rooms or Henry from paying Krell the £50. Rather, its effect was to deprive one party entirely of the benefit he expected from the other's performance, since it made the use of Krell's rooms during the period for which they were let virtually worthless to Henry. In general, the doctrine of impracticability of performance operates to the advantage of parties that are bound to furnish goods, land, services, or some similar performance, while the doctrine of frustration of purpose operates to the advantage of parties that are to pay money in return for those performances.

The doctrine of frustration has been generally accepted by American courts. Although the doctrine is not explicitly recognized by the Uniform Commercial Code, there is little doubt that it is applicable to contracts for the sale of goods.

The Restatement Second synthesis of the doctrine of frustration of purpose is strikingly similar to that of the doctrine of impracticability of performance. The party that claims that a supervening event frustrated its purpose must meet four requirements, only the first of which is different from those for impracticability. First, the event must have "substantially frustrated" that party's "principal purpose." Second, it must have been "a basic assumption on which the contract was made" that the event would not occur. Third, the frustration must have resulted without the fault of the party seeking to be excused. Fourth, that party must not have assumed a greater obligation than the law imposes. In applying the doctrine of frustration, as in applying that of impossibility, courts have sometimes been reluctant to entrust the granting of excuse on this ground to a jury. Furthermore, despite the similarity of the requirements for the two doctrines, courts have been much more reluctant to hold that a party has been excused on the ground of frustration than on the ground of impracticability.

§ 9.9. Effects of Impracticability and Frustration. The effect of *supervening* impracticability or frustration on the excused party is usually to discharge that party's remaining duties of performance. The effect of *existing* impracticability or frustration on the excused party is usually to prevent any duty of performance on that party's side from arising.[…]

A prospective failure of performance due to impracticability or frustration has a similar effect. The fact that one party's anticipated failure to perform will be excused on the ground of impracticability or frustration does not prevent the other party from justifiably suspending performance and from terminating the contract. But the other party cannot recover damages for breach.[…]

Transatlantic Financing Corporation v. United States of America
(C.A.D.C. 1966, 363 F.2d 312)

J. SKELLY WRIGHT, Circuit Judge:

"The doctrine of impossibility of performance has gradually been freed from the earlier fictional and unrealistic strictures of such tests as the 'implied term' and the parties' 'contemplation.' It is now recognized that "A thing is impossible in legal contemplation when it is not practicable; and a thing is impracticable when it can only be done at an excessive and unreasonable cost." The doctrine ultimately represents the ever-shifting line, drawn by courts hopefully responsive to commercial practices and mores, at which the community's interest in having contracts enforced according to their terms is outweighed by the commercial senselessness of requiring performance. When the issue is raised, the court is asked to construct a condition of performance based on the changed circumstances, a process which involves at least three reasonably definable steps. First, a contingency—something unexpected—must have occurred. Second, the risk of the unexpected occurrence must not have been allocated either by agreement or custom. Finally, occurrence of the contingency must have rendered performance commercially impracticable. Unless the court finds these three requirements satisfied, the plea of impossibility must fail."

C. International/Multinational

UNIDROIT

Article 6.2.1 (Contract to be observed)

Where the performance of a contract becomes more onerous for one of the parties, that party is nevertheless bound to perform its obligations subject to the following provisions on hardship.

Article 6.2.2 (Definition of hardship)

There is hardship where the occurrence of events fundamentally alters the equilibrium of the contract either because the cost of a party's performance has increased of because the value of the performance has increased or because the value of the performance a party receives has diminished, and

    (a) the events occur or become known to the disadvantaged party after the conclusion of the contract;

    (b) the events could not reasonably have been taken into account by the disadvantaged party at the time of the conclusion of the contract;

    (c) the events are beyond the control of the disadvantaged party; and

    (d) the risk of the events was not assumed by the disadvantaged party.

Article 6.2.3 (Effects of hardship)

(1) In case of hardship the disadvantaged party is entitled to request renegotiations. The request shall be made without undue delay and shall indicate the grounds on which it is based.

(2) The request for renegotiation does not in itself entitle the disadvantaged party to withhold performance.

(3) Upon failure to reach agreement within a reasonable time either party may resort to the court.

(4) If the court finds hardship it may, if reasonable,

(a) terminate the contract at a date and on terms to be fixed, or

(b) adapt the contract with a view to restoring its equilibrium.

Article 7.1.7 (Force majeure)

(1) Non-performance by a party is excused if that party proves that the non-performance was due to an impediment beyond its control and that it could not reasonably be expected to have taken the impediment into account at the time of the conclusion of the contract or to have avoided or overcome it or its consequences.

(2) When the impediment is only temporary, the excuse shall have effect for such period as is reasonable having regard to the effect of the impediment on the performance of the contract.

(3) The party who fails to perform must give notice to the other party of the impediment and its effect on its ability to perform. If the notice is not received by the other party within a reasonable time after the party who fails to perform knew or ought to have known of the impediment, it is liable for damages resulting from such nonreceipt.

(4) Nothing in this article prevents a party from exercising a right to terminate the contract or to withhold performance or request interest on money due.

Article 3. 3 (Initial impossibility)

(1) The mere fact that at the time of the conclusion of the contract the performance of the obligation assumed was impossible does not affect the validity of the contract.

(2) The mere fact that at the time of the conclusion of the contract a party was not entitled to dispose of the assets to which the contract relates does not affect the validity of the contract.

COMMENT

1. Performance impossible from the outset

Contrary to a number of legal systems which consider a contract of sale void if the specific goods sold have already perished at the time of conclusion of the contract, para. (1) of this article, in conformity with the most modern trends, states in general terms that the mere fact that at the time of the conclusion of the contract the performance of the obligation assumed was impossible does not affect the validity of the contract.

A contract is valid even if the assets to which it relates have already perished at the time of contracting, with the consequence that initial impossibility of performance is equated with impossibility occurring after the conclusion of the contract. The rights and duties of the parties arising from one party's (or possibly even both parties') inability to perform are to be determined according to the rules on non-performance.[…]

The rule laid down in para. (1) also removes possible doubts as to the validity of contracts for the delivery of future goods.[…]

Para. (1) moreover departs from the rule to be found in some civil law systems according to which the object (*objet*) of a contract must be possible.

The paragraph also deviates from the rule of the same systems which requires the existence of a *cause*, since, in a case of initial impossibility, the *cause* for a counter-performance is lacking.

Principles of European Contract Law

ARTICLE 4:102: INITIAL IMPOSSIBILITY

A contract is not invalid merely because at the time it was concluded performance of the obligation assumed was impossible, or because a party was not entitled to dispose of the assets to which the contract relates.

ARTICLE 6:111: CHANGE OF CIRCUMSTANCES

(1) A party is bound to fulfil its obligations even if performance has become more onerous, whether because the cost of performance has increased or because the value of the performance it receives has diminished.

(2) If, however, performance of the contract becomes excessively onerous because of a change of circumstances, the parties are bound to
enter into negotiations with a view to adapting the contract or ending it, provided that:

(a) the change of circumstances occurred after the time of conclusion of the contract,

(b) the possibility of a change of circumstances was not one which
could reasonably have been taken into account at the time of conclusion of the contract, and

(c) the risk of the change of circumstances is not one which, according to the contract, the party affected should be required to bear.

(3) If the parties fail to reach agreement within a reasonable period, the
court may:

(a) end the contract at a date and on terms to be determined by the
court; or

(b) adapt the contract in order to distribute between the parties in a
just and equitable manner the losses and gains resulting from the
change of circumstances.

ARTICLE 8:108: EXCUSE DUE TO AN IMPEDIMENT

(1) A party's non-performance is excused if it proves that it is due to an
impediment beyond its control and that it could not reasonably have
been expected to take the impediment into account at the time of
the conclusion of the contract, or to have avoided or overcome the
impediment or its consequences.

(2) Where the impediment is only temporary the excuse provided by
this Article has effect for the period during which the impediment
exists. However, if the delay amounts to a fundamental non-performance, the creditor may treat it as such.

(3) The non-performing party must ensure that notice of the impediment and of its effect on its ability to perform is received by the other
within a reasonable time after the non-performing party knew or
ought to have known of these circumstances. The other party is entitled to damages for any loss resulting from the non-receipt of such
notice.

CISG

Section IV. <u>Exemptions Article 79</u>

(1) A party is not liable for a failure to perform any of his obligations if he proves that the failure was due to an impediment beyond his control and that he could not reasonably be expected to have taken the impediment into account at the time of the conclusion of the contract or to have avoided or overcome it or its consequences.

(2) If the party's failure is due to the failure by a third person whom he has engaged to perform the whole or part of the contract, that party is exempt from liability only if:

(a) he is exempt under the preceding paragraph; and

(b) the person whom he has so engaged would be so exempt if the provisions of that paragraph were applied to him.

(3) The exemption provided by this article has effect for the period during which the impediment exists

(4) The party who fails to perform must give notice to the other party of the impediment and its effect on his ability to perform. If the notice is not received by the other party within a reasonable time after the party who fails to perform knew or ought to have known of the impediment, he is liable for damages resulting from such non-receipt.

(5) Nothing in this article prevents either party from exercising any right other than to claim damages under this Convention.

D. Courts' Decisions

1. Civil Law

France

Cour de cassation, 1ère Civ. 8 décembre 1998
Bull.1998 I n.346 p.238

Whereas, according to the contract of May 29, 1990, Castorama Inc, entrusted to ICEV Lid' air voyages Inc., the transportation and housing of five hundred members of its staff, from Jan. 21 to 24, 1991, to and in the city of Marrakech,...; whereas, after having contemplated cancelling the trip because of the tension in the Middle East and the Arab countries, Castorama Inc. declared, on Dec. 21, 1991, that the trip was on; whereas, on the 14th of Jan. 1991, on the eve of the Irak war, it cancelled the trip on "the ground of the worsening of the crisis in the Gulf"; whereas it requested reimbursement of the totality of the payments made to the travel agency claiming, in order to justify its unilateral breach of the contract, force majeure due to the war in the Gulf;

Whereas Castorama Inc. criticizes the court decision under appeal (Paris, April 12, 1996 ...) for having held that the circumstances raised were neither unforeseeable nor inevitable, and that by considering the impact of the Gulf war on this litigation only in Jan. 1991 without attempting to find out if, on the day of the perfection of the contract, Castorama Inc. could have reasonably foreseen the occurrence of that event, the Court of Appeal failed to provide a legal basis for its decision in relation to article 1148 of the civil Code; ...

But whereas, the Court of Appeal, when it held that the circumstances claimed to amount to force majeure were not insurmountable, did, thereby, legally justified its decision ...

Whereas, besides, the Court of Appeal stated that the city of Marrakech and the kingdom of Morocco were not, in Jan. 1991, places with high risk of attacks..., and that the Ministry of Foreign Affairs had not listed Morocco as a country that French citizens should not visit.... ; the Court of Appeal did address the issues raised and dismissed them ...

Cour de cassation, ass. plén. 14 avril 2006
D. 2006 n.23 p.1577

[facts omitted]

But considering that no payment of damages is owed when, because of either force majeure or fortuitous event (cas fortuit), the debtor was prevented to give or do that which he had bound himself to give or do, or did what he was prohibited from doing; that such is the case when the debtor was prevented to perform because of illness, to the extent that this event, being unforeseeable at the time of perfection of the contract and irresistible in its performance, is tantamount to a case of force majeure; [the debtor did die of his illness].... the Court of Appeal was correct in holding that these circumstances amounted to a case of force majeure..

Québec

Canit Construction Québec Limited et Janin & Compagnie Limitée v. The Foundation Company of Canada Ltd.
[1972] C.A. 81

[Facts, summary : Canit-Janin Inc. abandoned their attempt to build a harbor in Port Cartier after they had done a substantial amount of work. Foundation took over the work of excavation for the benefit of Québec Cartier Mining Company. Foundation leased three shovels from Canin; two big ones and a smaller shovel. The contract of lease, dated Nov.1960, included several provisions but one dealt specifically with force majeure: '3: The Foundation Company ... reserves the right to nullify the 2,000 hours guarantee if Canit-Janin are unable to provided shovel/dragline in working condition for more than one week. If it should become necessary or in case of force majeure on the part of the Foundation Company..., to cancel this agreement prior to the expiration of the 2,000 hours guarantee, The Foundation Company ... will pay the balance of hours ... at 50% of operating hour rate.' In Dec. 1960 the two big shovels were destroyed by a storm of unusual strength and became useless; the smaller shovel became the object of a new lease. In Aug.1965 Canit-Janin brought an action for payment of the leased shovels against Foundation that countered with the defense of force majeure]

M. le juge Brossard.... I have no doubt, as far as I am concerned, that the two main shovels have been destroyed by force majeure: to wit, the uncontrollable power shortage and the destructive force of the storm.... The destruction of the object made impossible, not only the obligation of Canit-Janin to ensure the proper functioning of the equipment, but also the actual use of the equipment by Foundation.... I think it is useful to cite, in extenso, the effect that the lower court judge gave to provision 3 of the contract: "[...] In other words, the clause assumes that the plaintiffs are in the position to fulfill their obligations but that for certain reasons applying to defendant, which are obscurely described, the defendant may cancel on paying the 50% rate. The destruction of the shovels by *force majeure* did not affect defendant alone but both parties equally because of their inextricably linked reciprocal obligations. The *force majeure* "on the part of defendant" in this clause is not the *force majeure* which produces, by the force of law alone, the cancellation of obligations. As the Court views it, the clause is not intended to express in a particular case what the law provides, but rather to give a right to defendant, which it would not otherwise have, to cancel the contract upon paying what may be described as a penalty or liquidated damages for the exercise of that right.

Germany

BGHZ 60, 14, VII. Civil Senate

(VII ZR 239/71) (engl. translation) in the web site
of The University of Texas School of Law[35]

On 30 January 1970 the defendant telephoned the plaintiff's travel agency and booked a package holiday in Tenerife for his five-member family from 5 to 19 February 1970 at a price of DM 5,142. The next day the defendant learnt that by reason of an outbreak of smallpox in Germany, the Spanish authorities had made entry to territory under Spanish sovereignty conditional on possession of a vaccination certificate. He consulted a doctor about his four-year old daughter who suffered from bronchitis, and the doctor advised that she should not be vaccinated, so on 2 February the defendant cancelled the booking. That very day the flight-organiser, T. GmbH & Co. XG, billed the plaintiff by so-called Stornogebllhr for DM 3,945. The plaintiff now claims payment of this sum with interest.

The Landgericht allowed the claim and the Oberlandes-gericht substantially dismissed the defendant's appeal. The defendant was given leave to appeal further, but that appeal is now dismissed.

Reasons

I. The Court of Appeal held that performance of the travel contract was rendered permanently impossible by the defendant's decision not to have his family vaccinated. The date and destination of the trip being fixed, performance of the contract could not be deferred. The plaintiff, however, could claim the proper fee under para. 324 par. 1 BGB since the defendant was responsible for the circumstance which rendered performance impossible. The area of responsibility of the respective parties under this provision was to be determined by the principle of good faith in relation to the purpose of the contract. In the case of a travel contract it is the traveller's business to see that he satisfies the personal requirements for the fulfilment of the trip, He and members of the family travelling with him must be in sufficient health to make the planned trip, and must also satisfy any health requirements in-

---

35. http://www.utexas.edu/law/academics/centers/transnational/work/,[Institute of Transnational Law, University of Texas at Austin].

volved. Thus although the defendant was not at fault in not letting his daughter be vaccinated, he was responsible for the obstacle to performance which her non-vaccination presented. The Court of Appeal held that the quantum of the plaintiff's claim was not yet ripe for determination, so it simply decided on its bien-fondé.

II. The appeal must be dismissed.

1. The Court of Appeal proceeded on the assumption that the contract between the parties was a contract of services (Werkvertrag). This accords with the prevalent view in the cases and is correct in law (references omitted).

2. The Court of Appeal was right to treat the travel contract between the parties as an absolutes Fixgeschäft (references omitted) where the time of performance is so critical that once it has passed, not only do the consequences spelled out in para. 361 BGB ensue, but performance becomes permanently impossible. Contrary to the view of the appellant, this is the case with a trip like the one here, which must take place within a specified period of time.

3. This case is one of subsequent impossibility, since the plaintiff's performance was rendered impossible by an event which occurred after the formation of the contract, namely the decision of the Spanish authorities that German tourists should not enter Spanish sovereign territory without proof of vaccination, and the refusal of the defendant to have his family vaccinated. This meant that they could not land on the island of Tenerife, which is Spanish.

4. The defendant is not to blame for this impossibility, since it is agreed that his child's acute bronchitis made her vaccination inadvisable. This affected the whole family, for the trip was an outing for the whole family of five and was booked as such. In a case like the present, the obstacle to performance, though inhering in only one of them, affected the whole family, especially as that one was a child of four. The defendant therefore cannot be blamed for having cancelled the whole trip, although vaccination was possible for everyone except the youngest daughter.

[...]

6. According to the Court of Appeal, it is not only blameworthy conduct a creditor 'is responsible for' under para. 324 par. 1 BGB, but any obstacle whatever to performance which falls within his 'area of risk.' In order to determine the area of risk within which a contractor is unconditionally responsible, one must examine the purpose of the particular contract in the light of

the principle of good faith. We need not decide how far, if at all, we can accept this view, for the obstacle to performance here in issue is covered by special provisions relating to contracts of services.

[...]

b) It might be possible to extrapolate from para. 644, 645 BGB and develop a theory of 'spheres' which one could apply quite generally to contracts of services [...]All we are doing here is to apply para. 645 par. 1 sent. 1 BGB to a particular set of facts, as we have done before in a case where the interests of the parties so required (see BGHZ 4O, 7t).

[...] Here it was an act of the customer, namely his decision not to have his family vaccinated, which made it impossible to carry out the work, here the trip. Neither here nor in BGHZ 40,71 was there any question of fault on the part of the customer.

c)[...]

d)[...] the idea behind the rule in the Code is an equitable one, effecting a reconciliation of the conflicting interests which is acceptable to both parties. Whereas under para. 323 BGB it is the contractor, and under para. 324 BGB the customer, that bears the entire risk of the fee, para. 645 par. 1 sent. 1 BGB by contrast leaves the customer with the disadvantage involved in the loss, deterioration or impossibility of the service due to some defect in the material, but it refrains from adding the further burden of his having to pay for the loss the contractor suffers through not being able to carry out the work (which is the practical effect of para. 324 BGB). When such a 'misfortune' strikes the customer, the contractor must rest content with compensation for the services he has already performed, plus an indemnity for his expenses.

These considerations are equally in point when the service has become incapable of performance because a person is no longer able, for reasons for which he is not responsible, to co-operate as required. This is quite clear in cases like the present. When the defendant booked the journey for himself and his family, there were no entry requirements for Spain. The subsequent ordinance by the Spanish authorities was an event which lay outside the sphere of direct influence of both parties, and struck them both. As a result, the defendant's four-year old daughter, and thus the entire family, became unfit for the journey which the plaintiff had booked. However one delimits the area of risk of the respective parties to a travel contract, this was a 'misfortune' for the defendant in the sense that the plaintiff must bear some of the consequences in accordance with the equitable principle underlying para.

645 par. 1 sent. 1 BGB. If it had already been known that proof of vaccination was required for entry to Spain, the defendant would never have contracted with the plaintiff at all, and then the plaintiff would have received nothing whatever. As it is, the plaintiff obtains at any rate an equitable sum for the services it had already rendered and compensation for any expenses it had incurred. This being the case where neither party could have foreseen the obstacle to the carrying out of the journey booked by the defendant, the result does justice to the interests of both parties, and answers the requirements of equity as expressed by the legislator in para. 645 par. 1 sent. 1 BGB for similar cases III. In all probability the plaintiff has a claim for some sum against the defendant, so we must uphold the judgment of the Court of Appeal that the claim is well-founded. The Court of Appeal must now determine the amount to which the plaintiff is entitled,[...]

BGH NJW 1984, 1746, VIII. Civil Senate

(engl. translation) in the web site of The University of Texas School of Law[36]

Facts

In 1977 the plaintiff, an Iranian importer, ordered from the defendant, a German brewery, 12,000 cases of export beer, 24 cans per case, at a price of DM 15.36 per case. The price of DM 184,320 was paid by draft on a bank in Teheran in July 1977. The goods were to be delivered c.i.f. Teheran, and were shipped in August 1977 from Bremen to a port in Iran, whence they were largely distributed inland. Investigations disclosed that about 40% of the goods were damaged and unusable, and on 7 November 1978 the parties reached the following compromise: "Until 31 May 1980 the plaintiff may buy cases of beer at a reduced price of DM 9.30 ... Payment of DM 20,000 will shortly be made to the plaintiff's account in Teheran. The balance of the sum demanded as damages, a further DM 20,000, will be paid on receipt of a draft in respect of 20,000 cases of beer ..." The first DM 20,000 was paid to the plaintiff by the defendant, but no more deliveries of beer were made nor was the further DM 20,000 paid to the plaintiff. In January 1979 the Shah fled and Ayatollah Khomeini seized power in Iran. Since then, according to the plaintiff, the Islamic Republic has a total prohibition, on pain of death, of trade in alcoholic products and the importation of al-

---

36. http://www.utexas.edu/law/academics/centers/transnational/work/,[Institute of Transnational Law, University of Texas at Austin].

cohol into Iran. The plaintiff wished to negotiate a further extra judicial settlement, but the defendant would not consent, so the plaintiff in the present litigation claimed damages in respect of the useless beer in the amount of DM 53,728 (i.e. 40% of DM 184,320 = DM 73,728 less DM 20,000 already received).

The Landgericht gave judgment for the full amount, the Oberlandesgericht only in the sum of DM 37,000. The [defendant's] appeal was dismissed.

Reasons

II.

1....

c) According to the court below, this was not a case of impossibility of performance, since the prohibition of importing alcohol into Iran did not affect the defendant's duty to make compensation for the harm it had caused. The parties do not challenge this, and the court was correct so to hold, at any rate in the result, since the plaintiff's obligations under the compromise were performed by the very act of making it (partial release, granting of delay, modification of the debt) and the defendant's obligations there under, namely to pay the further DM 20,000 and to deliver discounted beer f.o.b. German ports as agreed in 1977, were perfectly capable of being performed. The plaintiff was not bound to order any beer or to set up a credit line; these were options of the plaintiff and preconditions of the defendant's obligations.

d) The court below was right—as the parties accept—to deny that the compromise was invalidated by para. 779 BGB. Under this provision a compromise is invalid only when the actual underlying facts differed from those supposed by the parties. If, by contrast, expectations as to future events which the parties entertained at the time of the compromise are falsified by subsequent occurrences—such as here the political developments in Iran and their effect on the contract—para. 779 BGB cannot invalidate the compromise [references].

e) The court below was correct to start from the position that the basis of the transaction [Geschäftsgrundlage] of 7 November 1978 subsequently collapsed.

aa) Even the appellant admits that, quite apart from para. 779 BGB, para. 242 BGB is applicable to a compromise. [reference].

bb) The basis of a transaction consists of the common assumptions entertained by the parties at the time of the contract, or of an assumption of one of the parties, ascertainable by the other and not objected to by him, regarding the existence or future occurrence of circumstances, to the extent that the parties' intention to make the transaction is based on such assumptions [reference]. The court below held that the possibility of further deals between the parties was the basis of the transaction. The appellant's objection to this is misconceived. This was not simply a wish of the parties, even though it was frequently expressed, for only further dealings could achieve the economic purpose of the compromise, to make good the losses suffered by the plaintiff. The discount on the price of the beer could make sense only if the plaintiff could dispose of any beer it ordered. The finding that this assumption by the parties formed the basis of the compromise is not in conflict with the principle that a party may not, by invoking matters which fall within his own area of risk, claim that the basis of the transaction has collapsed [reference]. It is true that in commercial matters the risk of being unable to dispose of the goods normally falls within the purchaser's area of risk [reference], but the court below was right to point out that this was not a contract of sale but a transaction by which the defendant was to compensate the plaintiff for its losses. There is nothing to suggest that if the compensation envisaged by the compromise failed to materialise, the parties intended the loss to be borne by the plaintiff alone.

cc) The basis of the compromise has collapsed. The court below found that trade in alcoholic drinks in Iran is forbidden. The appellant's objections are without merit ...

dd) This court has always held that the collapse of the basis of a transaction can only be invoked when otherwise there would be manifestly intolerable consequences inconsistent with law and justice and such as cannot be imputed to the party affected [references]. Nevertheless, the basis of a transaction may be held to have collapsed if the balance of the reciprocal obligations has been gravely disturbed by some intervening event [reference]. In this compromise the plaintiff, in return for waiving its right to sue in respect of the delivery of defective beer in August 1977, was to receive a given benefit in exchange, and is entitled to more than a fraction of that benefit.

The appellant objects in vain that the plaintiff should have foreseen the political developments in Iran. The parties' expectations—here of their future cooperation—may constitute the basis of a transaction even if they are aware that their expectations may not be answered. According to the findings of the court below, to which the appellant makes no procedural objections, the possibility that these expectations might be frustrated was not so manifest as to prevent the plaintiff from invoking the collapse of the basis of the transaction.

ee) Notwithstanding the collapse of the basis of the transaction, the court below upheld the compromise, but altered its terms. It was right to do so [references]. Only exceptionally do the rules of collapse of the basis of the transaction make the contract disappear in toto; the general rule is that the contract should be maintained so far as possible and simply adjusted to the changed situation so as to do justice to the justified interests of both parties [references.] The evidence does not suggest that if they had known how matters would develop, the parties would have refused to enter any compromise at all. After all, when the plaintiff notified him that the goods were defective, the defendant originally proposed a deal which made no reference whatever to further deliveries of beer. If the compromise is to be upheld, the prior legal situation is irrelevant, so it is immaterial how seriously the defendant questioned the size of the plaintiff's claim or whether or not the compromise was a very generous one on his part.

The way the court below set about adapting the contractual duties of the parties to the altered circumstances represents an exercise of an ex officio discretion of the judge of fact [reference]. The court divided the loss resulting from the collapse of the basis of the transaction equally between the parties. […]

2. Common Law

U.S.A.

American Trading and Production Corporation v. Shell International Marine Ltd.
453 F.2d 939, 1972 A.M.C. 318

MULLIGAN, Circuit Judge:

The owner is a Maryland corporation doing business in New York and the charterer is a United Kingdom corporation. On March 23, 1967 the parties entered into a contract of voyage charter in New York City which provided that the charterer would hire the owner's tank vessel, WASHINGTON TRADER, for a voyage with a full cargo of lube oil from Beaumont/Smiths Bluff, Texas to Bombay, India. The charter party provided that the freight rate would be in accordance with the then prevailing American Tanker Rate Schedule (ATRS), […] and in addition there was a charge of $.85 per long ton for passage through the Suez Canal. On May 15, 1967 the WASHINGTON TRADER departed from Beaumont […]. The charterer paid the freight at the invoiced sum of $417,327.36 on May 26, 1967. […] On June

5th the owner cabled the ship's master advising him of various reports of trouble in the Canal and suggested delay in entering it pending clarification. On that very day, the Suez Canal was closed due to the state of war which had developed in the Middle East. The owner then communicated with the charterer on June 5th [...] requesting approval for the diversion of the WASHINGTON TRADER [...]. On June 6th the charterer responded that under the circumstances it was "for owner to decide whether to continue to wait or make the alternative passage via the Cape since Charter Party Obliges them to deliver cargo without qualification." In response the owner replied on the same day that in view of the closing of the Suez, the WASHINGTON TRADER would proceed to Bombay via the Cape of Good Hope and "[w]e [are] reserving all rights for extra compensation." The vessel proceeded westward, back through the Straits of Gibraltar and around the Cape and eventually arrived in Bombay on July 15th (some 30 days later than initially expected), traveling a total of 18,055 miles instead of the 9,709 miles [...]. The owner billed $131,978.44 as extra compensation which the charterer has refused to pay.

[...] the owner argues that transit of the Suez Canal was the agreed specific means of performance of the voyage charter and that the supervening destruction of this means rendered the contract legally impossible to perform and therefore discharged the owner's unperformed obligation. Consequently, when the WASHINGTON TRADER eventually delivered the oil after journeying around the Cape of Good Hope, a benefit was conferred upon the charterer for which it should respond in *quantum meruit*. The validity of this proposition depends upon a finding that the parties contemplated or agreed that the Suez passage was to be the exclusive method of performance [...]. We cannot construe the agreement in such a fashion. The parties contracted for the shipment of the cargo from Texas to India at an agreed rate and the charter party makes absolutely no reference to any fixed route. [...] In our view [...] both parties contemplated that the Canal would be the probable route. It was the cheapest and shortest, and therefore it was in the interest of both that it be utilized. However, this is not at all equivalent to an agreement that it be the exclusive method of performance. The charter party does not so provide and it seems to have been well understood in the shipping industry that the Cape route is an acceptable alternative in voyages of this character.[...]

This leaves us with the question as to whether the owner was excused from performance on the theory of commercial impracticability. Even though the owner is not excused because of strict impossibility, it is urged that American law recognizes that performance is rendered impossible if it can only be accomplished with extreme and unreasonable difficulty, expense, injury or loss. There is no extreme or unreasonable difficulty apparent here. [...] The owner's case here essentially rests upon the element of the additional expense involved—$131,978.44. This represents an increase of less than one third over the agreed upon $417,327.36. We find that this increase in expense is not sufficient to constitute commercial impracticability under either American or English authority.[...]

Mere increase in cost alone is not a sufficient excuse for non-performance[...]. It must be an "extreme and unreasonable" expense[...]

Matters involving impossibility or impracticability of performance of contract are concededly vexing and difficult. One is even urged on the allocation of such risks to pray for the "wisdom of Solomon." 6 A. Corbin, Contracts § 1333, at 372 (1962). On the basis of all of the facts, the pertinent authority and a further belief in the efficacy of prayer, we affirm.

Mishara Construction Company, Inc. v. Transit-Mixed Concrete Corp.

365 Mass. 122, 310 N.E. 2d 363, 1974

REARDON, Justice.

The plaintiff Mishara Construction Company, Inc. (Mishara) was the general contractor [...] for the construction of Rose Manor, a housing project [...]. In September, 1966, the plaintiff negotiated with the defendant Transit-Mixed Concrete Corp. (Transit) for the supplying of ready-mixed concrete to be used on the project. [...] Transit would supply all the concrete needed on the project at a price of $13.25 a cubic yard, with deliveries to be made at the times and in the amounts as ordered by Mishara. [...] Performance under this contract was satisfactory to both parties until April, 1967. In that month a labor dispute disrupted work on the job site. Although work resumed on June 15, 1967, a picket line was maintained on the site until the completion of the project in 1969. Throughout this period, with very few exceptions, no deliveries of concrete were made by Transit notwithstanding frequent requests by Mishara. After notifying Transit of its intention, Mishara purchased the balance of its concrete requirements elsewhere. Mishara sought in damages the additional cost of concrete incurred by virtue of the higher price of the replacement product[...]

The excuse of impossibility in contracts for the sale of goods is controlled by the appropriate section of the Uniform Commercial Code, G.L. c. 106, s 2-615. That section sets up two requirements before performance may be excused. First, the performance must have become 'impracticable.' Second, the impracticability must have been caused 'by the occurrence of a contingency the non-occurrence of which was a basic assumption on which the contract was made.'[...]

By adopting the term 'impracticability' rather than 'impossibility' the drafters of the Code appear to be in accord with Professor Williston who stated that 'the essence of the modern defense of impossibility is that the promised performance was at the making of the contract, or thereafter became, impracticable owing to some extreme or unreasonable difficulty, expense, injury, or loss involved, rather than that it is scientifically or actually impossible.'[...]

It is implicit in the doctrine of impossibility (and the companion rule of 'frustration of purpose') that certain risks are so unusual and have such severe consequences that they must have been beyond the scope of the assignment of risks inherent in the contract, that is, beyond the agreement made by the parties. To require performance in that case would be to grant the promisee an advantage for which he could not be said to have bargained in making the contract.[...]The question is, given the commercial circumstances in which the parties dealt: Was the contingency which developed one which the parties could reasonably be thought to have foreseen as a real possibility which could affect performance? Was it one of that variety of risks which the parties were tacitly assigning to the promisor by their failure to provide for it explicitly? If it were, performance will be required. If it could not be so considered, performance is excused.[...]

[...]we consider Mishara's contention that a labor dispute which makes performance more difficult never constitutes an excuse for nonperformance. We think it is evident that in some situations a labor dispute would not meet the requirements for impossibility discussed above. A picket line might constitute a mere inconvenience and hardly make performance 'impracticable.'[...]Certainly, in general, labor disputes cannot be considered extraordinary in the course of modern commerce. [...] Much must depend on the facts known to the parties at the time of contracting with respect to the history of and prospects for labor difficulties during the period of performance of the contract, as well as the likely severity of the effect of such disputes on the ability to perform. [...] Where the probability of a labor dispute appears to be practically nil, and where the occurrence of such a dispute provides unusual difficulty, the excuse of impracticability might well be applicable.[...]

U.K.

Taylor and Another v. Caldwell and Another
3B. &S. 826, 1863

The judgment of the court was now delivered by

BLACKBURN J. In this case the plaintiffs and defendants had, on the 27th May, 1861, entered into a contract by which the defendants agreed to let the plaintiffs have the use of The Surrey Gardens and Music Hall on four days then to come, [...] for the purpose of giving a series of four grand concerts, and day and night fêtes at the Gardens and Hall on those days respectively; and the plaintiffs agreed to take the Gardens and Hall on those days, and pay 100l. for each day.[...]

The effect of the whole is to shew that the existence of the Music Hall in the Surrey Gardens in a state fit for a concert was essential for the fulfilment of the contract, such entertainments as the parties contemplated in their agreement could not be given without it.

After the making of the agreement, and before the first day on which a concert was to be given, the Hall was destroyed by fire. This destruction, we must take it on the evidence, was without the fault of either party, and was so complete that in consequence the concerts could not be given as intended. And the question we have to decide is whether, under these circumstances, the loss which the plaintiffs have sustained is to fall upon the defendants. The parties when framing their agreement evidently had not present to their minds the possibility of such a disaster, and have made no express stipulation with reference to it, so that the answer to the question must depend upon the general rules of law applicable to such a contract.

There seems no doubt that where there is a positive contract to do a thing, not in itself unlawful, the contractor must perform it or pay damages for not doing it, although in consequence of unforeseen accidents, the performance of his contract has become unexpectedly burthensome or even impossible.[...] But this rule is only applicable when the contract is positive and absolute, and not subject to any condition either express or implied: [...] in the absence of any express or implied warranty that the thing shall exist, the contract is not to be construed as a positive contract, but as subject to an implied condition that the parties shall be excused in case, before breach, performance becomes impossible from the perishing of the thing without default of the contractor. [...]

For in the course of affairs men in making such contracts in general would, if it were brought to their minds, say that there should be such a condition.

Accordingly, in the Civil law, such an exception is implied in every obligation of the class which they call obligatio de certo corpore. The rule is laid down in the Digest, lib. xLv., tit. l, de verborum obligationibus, 1. 33.[...] The principle is more fully developed in l. 23.[...] the principle is adopted in the Civil law as applicable to every obligation of which the subject is a certain thing. The general subject is treated of by Pothier[...]

Although the Civil law is not of itself authority in an English Court, it affords great assistance in investigating the principles on which the law is grounded. And it seems to us that the common law authorities establish that in such a contract the same condition of the continued existence of the thing is implied by English law. [...]

These are instances where the implied condition is of the life of a human being, but there are others in which the same implication is made as to the continued existence of a thing. For example, where a contract of sale is made amounting to a bargain and sale, transferring presently the property in specific chattels, which are to be delivered by the vendor at a future day; there, if the chattels, without the fault of the vendor, perish in the interval, the purchaser must pay the price and the vendor is excused from performing his contract to deliver, which has thus become impossible.

That this is the rule of the English law is established by the case of *Rugg v. Minett* (11 East, 210)[...]

This also is the rule in the Civil law[...]

The principle seems to us to be that, in contracts in which the performance depends on the continued existence of a given person or thing, a condition is implied that the impossibility of performance arising from the perishing of the person or thing shall excuse the performance. [...]In the present case, looking at the whole contract, we find that the parties contracted on the basis of the continued existence of the Music Hall at the time when the concerts were to be given; that being essential to their performance.[...]

Krell v. Henry

[1903] 2 KB 740

VAUGHAN WILLIAMS L.J.

[...]

The real question in this case is the extent of the application in English law of the principle of the Roman law which has been adopted and acted on in many English decisions, and notably in the case of Taylor v. Caldwell.[...] it is clear that the principle of the Roman law has been introduced into the English law. The doubt in the present case arises as to how far this principle extends. [...]English law applies the principle not only to cases where the performance of the contract becomes impossible by the cessation of existence of the thing which is the subject-matter of the contract, but also to cases where the event which renders the contract incapable of performance is the cessation or non-existence of an express condition or state of things, going to the root of the contract, and essential to its performance.[...]

I do not think that the principle of the civil law as introduced into the English law is limited to cases in which the event causing the impossibility of performance is the destruction or non-existence of some thing which is the subject-matter of the contract or of some condition or state of things expressly specified as a condition of it. I think that you first have to ascertain, [...] what is the substance of the contract, and then to ask the question whether that substantial contract needs for its foundation the assumption of the existence of a particular state of things. [...]The contract is contained in two letters of June 20 [...] These letters do not mention the coronation, but speak merely of the taking of Mr. Krell's chambers, or, rather, of the use of them, in the daytime of June 26 and 27, for the sum of 75l., 25l. then paid, balance 50l. to be paid on the 24th.[...] In my judgment the use of the rooms was let and taken for the purpose of seeing the Royal procession. It was not a demise of the rooms, or even an agreement to let and take the rooms. It is a licence to use rooms for a particular purpose and none other. And in my judgment the taking place of those processions on the days proclaimed along the proclaimed route, which passed 56A, Pall Mall, was regarded by both contracting parties as the foundation of the contract;[...] in the case of the coronation, there is not merely the purpose of the hirer to see the coronation procession, but it is the coronation procession and the relative position of the rooms which is the basis of the contract as much for the lessor as the hirer; and I think that if the King, before the coronation day and after the contract, had died, the hirer could not have insisted on having the rooms on the days named. [...]surely the view of the coronation procession was the foundation of the contract[...]Each case must be judged by its own circumstances. In each case one must ask oneself, first, what, having regard to all the circumstances, was the foundation of the contract? Secondly, was the performance of the contract prevented? Thirdly, was the event which prevented the performance of the contract of such a character that it cannot reasonably be said to have been in the contemplation of the parties at the date of the contract? If all these questions are answered in the affirmative (as I think they should be in this case), I think both parties are discharged from further performance of the contract.[...] The test seems to be whether the event which causes the impossibility was or might have been anticipated and guarded against.[...] In the present case the condition which fails and prevents the achievement of that which was, in the contemplation of both parties, the foundation of the contract, is not expressly mentioned either as a condition of the contract or the purpose of it; but I think for the reasons which I have given that the principle of Taylor v. Caldwell ought to be applied. This disposes of the plaintiff's claim for 50l. unpaid balance of the price agreed to be paid for the use of the rooms. The defendant at one time set up a cross-claim for the return of the 25l. he paid at the date of the contract. [...] I have only to add [...] that in the case of contracts falling directly within the rule of Taylor v. Caldwell the subsequent impossibility does not affect rights already acquired, because the defendant had the whole of June 24 to pay the balance, and the public announcement that the coronation and processions would not take place on the proclaimed days was made early on the morning of the 24th, and no cause of action could accrue till the end of that day. I think this appeal ought to be dismissed.[...]

Staffordshire Area Health Authority v. South Staffordshire Waterworks Co.
[1978] 1 W.L.R. 1387

LORD DENNING M.R. Four simple words "at all times hereafter" have given rise to this important case.[...]

Contracts which contain no provision for determination[...]

The cost of supply of goods and services goes up with inflation through the rooftops and the fixed payment goes down to the bottom of the well so that it is worth little or nothing. Rather than tolerate such inequality, the courts will construe the contract so as to hold that it is determinable by reasonable notice. [...]They say that in the circumstances as they have developed—which the parties never had in mind—the contract ceases to bind the parties forever. It can be determined on reasonable notice.[...]

Inflation

[...]We have [...] had mountainous inflation and the pound dropping to cavernous depths.[...]It seems to me that we have reached the point which Viscount Simon contemplated in *British Movietonews Ltd.* v. *London and Dis-*

trict Cinemas Ltd.[1952] A.C. 166, 185. Speaking à propos of a depreciation of currency, he envisaged a situation where

"a consideration of the terms of the contract, in the light of the circumstances existing when it was made, shows that they never agreed to be bound in a fundamentally different situation which has now unexpectedly emerged, ..."

Where such a situation emerges, he went on to say:

"the contract ceases to bind at that point—not because the court in its discretion thinks it just and reasonable to qualify the terms of the contract, but because on its true construction it does not apply to the situation."

[...]

So here the situation has changed so radically since the contract was made 50 years ago that the term of the contract "at all times hereafter" ceases to bind: and it is open to the court to hold that the contract is determined by reasonable notice.

Conclusion

I do not think that the water company could have determined the agreement immediately after it was made. That cannot have been intended by the parties. No rule of construction could sensibly permit such a result. But, in the past 50 years, the whole situation has changed so radically that one can say with confidence: "The parties never intended that the supply should be continued in these days at that price." Rather than force such unequal terms on the parties, the court should hold that the agreement could be and was properly determined in 1975 by the reasonable notice of six months.[...]

3. International/Multinational: CISG

Nuova Fucinati S.p.A. v. Fondmetal International A.B.
Tribunale Civile di Monza
Gius. It. 1994 I 145–150 [14.01.1993]

[Facts: An Italian seller and a Swedish buyer concluded in February 1988 a contract for the sale of 1,000 metric tons of metal (ferrochrome). The seller did not deliver the goods. The seller claimed avoidance of the contract for hardship ('eccessiva onerosità sopravvenuta') since the price of the goods had increased between the time of the conclusion of the contract and the time fixed for delivering by approximately 30%.][37]

[In the court's opinion, even if CISG had applied, the seller could not have relied on hardship as a ground for avoidance, as CISG does not contemplate this as a remedy either in Art. 79 or elsewhere. A domestic court could not integrate into CISG provisions of domestic law granting avoidance for hardship, as hardship is not a matter which is expressly excluded from the scope of the Convention by Art. 4 CISG.].[38]

"In particular the Convention, to which both Italy and Sweden are parties establishes in art. 79 that the avoidance by a party for hardship with respect to whatever obligations can be determined by the test that such hardship is due to an impediment independent from that party's will and that said impediment could not reasonably be foreseen."[39]

---

37. http://www.unilex.info/case.cfm?pid=1&do=case&id=21&step=Abstract [8/2/2007].

38. *Id.*

39. Liberal translation by Vicenç Feliu, Foreign, Comparative and International Law Librarian, LSU Law Center.

Index